ACHIEVING EVERLASTING JOY

a Journey-Map

Ellen Spivey

Author House

AuthorHouse™
1663 Liberty Drive
Bloomington, IN 47403
www.authorhouse.com
Phone: 1-800-839-8640

First published by AuthorHouse   02/23/2011

ISBN: 978-1-4567-2742-0 (sc)
ISBN: 978-1-4567-2740-6 (hc)
ISBN: 978-1-4567-2741-3 (e-b)

Library of Congress Control Number: 2011901062

Printed in the United States of America

Any people depicted in stock imagery provided by Thinkstock are models, and such images are being used for illustrative purposes only. Certain stock imagery © Thinkstock.

This book is printed on acid-free paper.

DEDICATION

To "Old One Who Is Wise", Ancient Inca Medicine Woman

With gratitude for her wisdom and guidance.

TABLE OF CONTENTS

INTRODUCTION

Little did I suspect the day that I opened my front door and my oldest friend, Mary Grove, stood there with a huge used canvas, that this would be the beginning of a long and great adventure. Mary was always on the lookout for inexpensive art materials for me, and this one was wall-sized. It had a painting of a beige orchid already on it with a beige background and a lovely bamboo style frame. The only problem was a ridge of raised paint outlining the orchid. There was no way I could see to take that outline away without tearing the canvas.

Several times I tried to put something on the canvas that would hide or detract from the raised ridges. Nothing that I painted was satisfactory to me, so I set the incomplete work aside for a time. In the meantime I moved to North Carolina. One day I decided to get my creative juices flowing and got the canvas out and my paints gathered around me on the floor. It was too large for my easel so I parked it against the wall, plopped down on the kitchen tile, and started fooling around to see what happened. In just a few moments the shape of a face appeared, and it looked and felt right and real. It was clearly an Indian woman's face, yet I had no idea where it had come from.

I put a collage of colors around the face and some flower petals which hid the raised lines on the canvas. I hung it behind my sofa and it covered most of the entire wall. A meditation group was meeting weekly at my house at the time, and when people came in they would tell me they were "drawn" into the eyes or were "mesmerized" by the painting. It never failed to elicit a response.

I didn't know anything more about the painting or who the Indian woman might be for probably two years or so. One fall day my friend Gordon Banta, who was a psychic and medium, and also channeled, (you will hear much more about him later on) was visiting. We were sitting on the sofa while he gave me a "reading" and after a while he said to me, "you know where this information is coming from don't you?" "No," I answered. He then told me it was coming from the woman in the painting!!!

I had always known that my paintings of people had what I called a "dynamic" that I didn't often see in other artists work, but this was a "first" for me. Gordon told me that the woman in the painting was an

Inca Indian Medicine woman who lived back in the 12th or 13th century. He told me her tribe named her when she was 28 years of age, "Old One Who Is Wise". He stated that she was revered by her people and spent her life developing her spirituality, and never married for that reason. Her people carried her everywhere she went because of their love and respect for her. "Old One Who Is Wise" also predicted things, like the airplane, which she called "the metal that flies". Gordon also told me that the chief of her tribe so honored her that he gave her a large emerald, which she wore in the middle of her forehead. And he said that she had been with my father during his lifetime, and would be with me from that time on.

Living in North Carolina, the gem capital of the world, I found an emerald of fair size which I purchased and placed in the center of her forehead as a way to honor her presence with me. I am sure it is not the quality of the original gem, yet I feel good about my gift to her. The painting now sits on the wall facing my bed, so she is very much with me every day.

I am certain that it is her spirit which led me to the Inca Medicine Wheel and to my writing of this book. It has been amazing to me to watch the progressive unfolding of the events from almost blank canvas to the finished product of this writing. It is clear to me that I have been guided to the resources needed and in the total process of the writing.

Last summer I went back to North Carolina for two months and found a lovely apartment attached to a Bed and Breakfast (High Haven Inn) outside of Franklin. It had a wonderful small and cozy porch overlooking woods, with an old-fashioned swing and rocking chairs. This is where I wrote the first draft of "ACHIEVING EVERLASTING JOY". I had started it several times previously and wasn't satisfied with it, yet I knew I would be ready for it at some time, and last summer was that time. It just flowed, and I was able to write almost without ceasing anytime I chose to do so. It is a work of love and it is a heritage for my children and grandchildren and to all those who are on their own spiritual journey.

My profession as a Clinical Social Worker has also contributed knowledge on the emotional levels as has my forty some years of providing psychotherapy for people of all ages and situations. I have always been growth oriented and used a growth model, even before I was aware of the Inca Medicine Wheel. My formal education included a BA, an MSW, and near completion of a double PhD in Health

Administration and Psychology. I completed everything except the writing of the dissertation. When I reached that point I decided I really didn't want to spend my life at that place in time working on writing for weeks and months. I had learned what I wanted to know.

I wish to know you heart to heart, without the separations of race, sex, education, etc. It is my hope to meet you, my readers, in the seminars I am beginning, on my email, or face to face; if not in this world then in the next dimension.

If you are like most people on your personal journey you may want to read this book, or parts of it, many times. Each time you will find something different, something more meaningful than when you first read it. You will also probably go backward, as well as forward, as new issues come to your consciousness. Honor your process. Embrace yourself wholly, and when you finally reach the emotional level where you can feel the lonely, suffering child who is so vulnerable, sensitive and very beautiful, you will want to comfort that small being with your whole heart. Never give up.!! You deserve those hugs and being held!!!! Allow the tears of JOY to flow and EMBRACE, EMBRACE, EMBRACE!!!!!

Every day can be an exciting adventure waiting to happen! Old One Who Is Wise, and I, send you forth on the greatest, most exhilarating journey imaginable and wish for you everlasting JOY!!!!!!!!!!!!!

EMBRACE YOURSELF

HUG YOURSELF MUCH

LEARN TO LOVE YOURSELF UNCONDITIONALLY

GIVE YOURSELF GIFTS EVERYDAY

KNOW THAT GOD IS LOVE

BE GENTLE TO YOURSELF

TREAT YOURSELF KINDLY

REACH FOR THE STARS

EVERLASTING JOY SHALL BE YOURS

THE INCA MEDICINE WHEEL

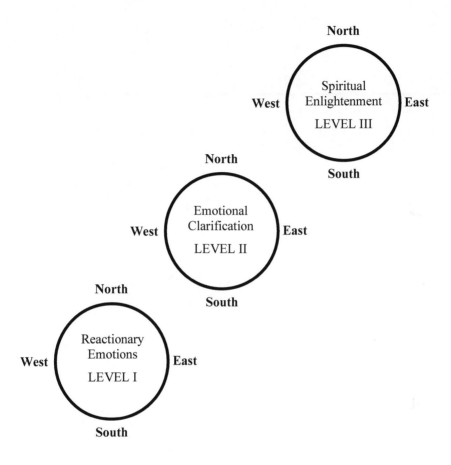

Directions to the Inca Medicine Wheel correspond to issues for each direction on every level:

South from the Wounded Self to Healer

West from Wounded Warrior to Compassionate Warrior

North from Emotional Chaos to Enlightenment

East from Judgment to Unconditional Love

LEVELS I, II, III

PART ONE

Essence and Definition

Everlasting, eternal JOY is not only our birthright, our inheritance as human beings, but our eventual destination. Wherever we are on our individual journeys, it is our evolutionary process to ultimately find lasting JOY. The good news is that we can make it happen. JOY is based on the personal vibrations each of us possesses. Each person's vibration is uniquely their own and ranges from the most dense in the "Root" chakra to the finest and lightest in the "Crown" chakra and above. The highest chakras are associated with JOY and bliss. Blockages prevent us from a smooth flow of energy from one chakra to another and from being able to live in the higher levels of being. It is possible to reach those highest vibratory energies where we live in that rarefied JOY FULL state. Our task at this time in history is to create of our lives, tapestries and mosaics of JOY!!!!! JOY is a higher vibration than even unconditional love, yet unconditional love is always a component of JOY.

I will give you a journey-map of how to achieve eternal JOY in this writing. It will help you remove the blockages of negative energy that prevent emotional health and JOY. That is not to say that it is an easy journey as it takes time, patience, and commitment. It takes the willingness to become aware of the heights and depths of our conscious and subconscious processes. We can learn to access these unknown parts of ourselves that are hidden from our awareness as we learn to accept and embrace more and more of who we really are.

JOY is who we really are. Definitions of the word, however, are rather sketchy. There are not many "J" words in the dictionary compared to other letters in the alphabet. JOY is not defined with any precision or carefulness. The meanings are stated as "strong feelings of pleasure, gladness, happiness, or outward rejoicing". It is synonymous with "rapture, bliss, delight". A bit better. Roget's Thesaurus adds a little more thoroughness with definitions of "enchantment, paradise, and exaltation". Even these lack refinement and depth. There is nothing about "inner" experience. When I think of, and/or experience JOY, it is an internal knowing, and it is felt as laughter that bubbles over, as well as singing and dancing. It is feeling fully alive. It is also a learning to trust deeply on many levels, and knowing that "home" in its truest sense is always in our own hearts. JOY is looking into the light and glory parts of ourselves and celebrating with great fullness. It is living right now; it is appreciating beauty in ourselves and our world. It is like sunrise with the promise of a new day, and it is like spring and knowing, without a doubt, that we are as important as anyone in the universe. I am also sure that love is JOY is love is JOY and that JOY is the epiphany, as well as the sure knowing in the deepest part of our beings that we were created in love, we are beloved, and we are unconditional love now and all ways and will be through all eternity. WE ARE JOY!!!!!

Everlasting JOY is also being aware that when there are other feelings predominate at the moment, that we still can feel the JOY "humming" away underneath everything else. We will still continue to experience a whole range of emotions, for it would be inappropriate to be grinning and acting JOYFUL in the face of somebody's tragedy. The knowing that it is there and that we can "tap" into it is what makes the difference.

When I began my journey I was unaware of any kind of guides, books, or counselors to help me on my path. When I was in high school I was wondering why I was the way I was. I would search through my sister's nursing text books to try to find answers, but there were none. I began my own passage and later found aid along the way. I think it will be faster for you than it has been for me to reach everlasting JOY. Today there is a voluminous supply of resources available, both emotional and spiritual, and they both lead to the same goal. If you choose this journey, there are compassionate hands and hearts that you may reach out to.

A few years ago while I was living in North Carolina, I was told about a book which describes an Inca Indian Medicine Wheel. The Wheel is multidimensional and has three levels. It dates back centuries ago and on two levels is very similar to the one I just sort of stumbled upon, or perhaps was led to on my own journey. In this text the Wheel is shown as one dimensional, yet I am convinced that in actuality it is a spiral similar to our own DNA helix. The spiral is an ancient symbol of birth and rebirth. The Inca Medicine Wheel[1] is the heritage of an educated and intelligent civilization with insights that, in my opinion, have surpassed modern day psychological precepts in clarity, leaving an easily understood, yet complex model that explains the full development of human potential[2].

Every once in a while, something comes along that is pure dynamite. It is so with the material in this small but potent book. It is about inspiration, psychology, spirituality and self growth. It is not a therapy per se, yet it is more than the sum total of all of the above.

In actuality, it is a softer, more compassionate, transforming way of life and living, perceived by the wisdom of the ancient Peruvian Inca Indians, wide open both emotionally and spiritually with a sophistication not realized in our so-called modern society.

It is a book for people like you and me who are serious about wanting and finding everlasting JOY without the pressures of competition, hierarchy and aggression. It is a gentle pathway to alignment with sacred consciousness and the realization of the divine within the inner being.

I will go into the teachings of the Inca Medicine Wheel in the third part of this book. What causes it to be so unique, are not only the three levels of the wheel, but the spiritual part of the paradigm. It is the most complete picture of the sequence of issues and actions to be taken for resolution of spiritual growth that I have found in over forty years of providing psychotherapy for people. It flows together as a total emotional/spiritual guide and one may begin wherever they are on their own pathway. One may also go backward or forward on levels as different issues arise. The description of the Inca Medicine Wheel in Part IV is my interpretation and experience of it. I am still working on the final level and I will lead you as far as I have gone, and as far as I can see.

Before we go any further I wanted to tell you that the words "accept" and "embrace" will be used interchangeably in this writing. However, I use the word "embrace" most often because the connotations for "embrace" are so much more representative of what I would like for all of us as an experience.

The synonyms for embrace are "to love, hug, feel natural affection for, to give kindness, tenderness to". This is what we so desperately need to bestow upon ourselves, all day, every day. We don't need to beat ourselves up. It simply doesn't work. All it does is to make us feel worse about ourselves. WE NEED TO LOVE OURSELVES JUST THE WAY WE ARE IN THIS VERY MOMENT!!!!!!!!

Acceptance has been the word used in our culture most often in terms of personal growth and it is a good word and is defined as the act of receiving something graciously, to take as satisfactory, to approve of. Not anywhere near as loving and caring a word as embrace. Start telling yourself every day, "I am embraceable, I am huggable!!!!!!!!" Sounds terrific, doesn't it, in comparison with "I am acceptable?" This is the kind of feeling quality I would like to see everyone develop for themselves.

Before I move ahead I wanted to mention that Part II of this writing is about emotions and issues that are common to most persons as they navigate their life journey. They are all subjects that I believe are particularly important. They may not be major issues for you in particular and if not, just disregard them.

Herstory

I was born in Pittsburgh, Pennsylvania during the latter days of the great depression. My parents made it through okay, but there were some tough times. They were bridge players, and usually played every weekend with friends. They often had no refreshments to serve except for saltine crackers. They were able to laugh about it later. My parents were products of their generation in some ways, but in many ways they were much more "open" than most of their peers. They had plenty of the hang-ups and neuroses that most people carried around with them. They talked to each other a lot, and home was usually a pleasant place to be. Their whole lives they were affectionate with one another. I was blessed in many ways.

To fill you in about my background, my maternal grandfather was a Director for the YMCA his entire adult life. My mother had grown up in a home that was youth oriented. The YMCA philosophy advocated good, clean fun and that was the way she was brought up. My granddad was quite modern in his thinking in that he believed the human body to be beautiful. He would go out to the middle of a lake and take off his shirt, which wasn't done in those days. He also believed that in the future, people wouldn't hide their bodies in layers and layers of clothing. This grandfather died before I was born so I never got to know him, yet his life and thinking definitely impacted mine.

He had no training in medicine, that I am aware of, yet he kept a little black bag (like old-time physicians), that my mother held onto after his death. I can remember digging it out of the attic and opening it to see what was in it. There were a few old medicine type bottles, but what I remember most were the odors of old musty herbs, and smelling salts, and other indeterminable aromas that were intriguing and mysterious. This was my only physical connection to this grandfather and I wondered about what he would have been like with me. if he had lived.

My grandmother, his wife, was quiet, as I remember her and she was a little thing. When I was seven years old I was taller than she was. I recall her holding on to my arm and leaning on me for support. She lived with us after my grandfather died, and when I was very small she took care of me more than my mother did. She would always stay with me at night until I went to sleep and I knew she loved me. She had abdominal cancer which was in remission for a few years. I was unaware she had it until it recurred after I was hurt in an accident riding my sister's bike.

My parents were out visiting friends when it happened. My sister, Marcia, who was exactly six years older than I (I was born on her birthday), was holding on to the bike while I rode, and I got away from her. I turned down a street that had a long hill and was almost through a big intersection when I was hit by a truck, which didn't stop. My sister stayed with me as I lay unconscious and bleeding in the street. After a few hours someone (not an ambulance) picked me up off the street and took me to a hospital. Marcia went with us and some neighborhood children went to my house and told my grandmother I was hurt and they didn't know if I was still alive or not. We had just moved to Washington, D.C. two weeks earlier. While all this was happening my mother had a premonition that I had been hurt and had my dad take them home. They didn't have any idea what hospital I was in, and it took them a while to find out. I clearly remember sitting up in the hospital bed with bandages on my head, a very extended and black eye and loose front teeth with a flap cut in my lower lip where my teeth had gone through it. I was making jokes because I could see how distraught they were and I felt bad for them. My grandmother never got over the shock and her cancer started growing. The accident happened in the fall—September I think—and Christmas day was the last time my grandmother was able to come downstairs or leave her room.

I was badly injured and bacteria from the street got into my kidneys from the gashes on my body. There were no antibiotics then. It was about six or seven more years before penicillin was discovered, or on the market. I can remember my fever being so high that my mom spent hours putting cold compresses all over me to bring my temperature down. I would beg her to keep cold cloths on my feet because they would be burning up. I had no control over my bladder. Ordinarily I would have been mortified by that, but I was too sick to care.

The good thing that I recall from that long term illness was that my dad would come in to see me when he came home from work. I looked forward to his visits each day. He would tell me stories about King Arthur and the Knights of the Round Table and he would have Sir Galahad riding a motorcycle and eating chocolate ice cream cones (which he knew I loved). I looked forward to those special times with my dad, as he would keep me laughing. It was six weeks before I was well enough to get out of bed and I was too weak to walk when I finally did. I was two months late starting school that year, but I quickly caught up as my reading skills were very good. My math was another thing altogether. I hated it. I remember both my mom and dad making me go over the times tables again and again. I would get so frustrated I would cry. I couldn't seem to keep my papers neat and would smear pencil marks all over them. The teacher would get provoked and fuss at me. I think there was just too much going on at home with my accident and my grandmother's terminal illness. I had severe headaches from the concussion I received, for about a year.

My mom had a hard time that fall and winter. She had no one to help her with my grandmother except my sister who had just turned fourteen in November, and she was in school all day. There was one neighbor who would come in briefly, from time to time, so mom could go get groceries. I don't think my dad was too much help except maybe in lifting my grandmother so the bed could be changed. I know mom was exhausted. One of the outstanding memories I have from that time concerned grammy's confusion. She was always thinking it was Sunday and wanting to know why my sister and I weren't dressed for Sunday school. Mom would ask us to go and put our Sunday clothes on and come into my grandmother's room and show her we were dressed for church. I don't recall if my sister balked, but I know I did. It seemed so foolish to me. I didn't want to stop my play or whatever I was doing, but I did, and it would satisfy grammy for a little while. She died in June the year I was eight, although it seemed she had died earlier because she wasn't there for me for several months.

My mother's childhood had revolved so much around young people's activities and having fun that she always encouraged Marcia and me to do the same. Our friends were always welcome at our house, and they all loved my parents. When I was in high school my friends always had their parties there because my mom enjoyed having kids around, and would roll up the rugs and push back the furniture. She always managed to get us away from town and in the country during the summertime. One year she rented a cottage in Pine Grove Furnace, Pennsylvania, and took several girls from Carlisle to take care of and chaperone so that we could have fun. She made enough money to pay the rent on the cottage, but it was hard work. She cooked huge meals as everyone would be starved from swimming and hiking and playing all day. She made sure we kids were safe and well.

Mom was also creative and could paint and write well. She wrote a couple of children's books but never got them published. One of them still brings tears to my eyes every time I read it. Another of my mother's qualities sticks with me over the years. Every afternoon before dad got home from work she would bathe and change into nice clothes. She always looked like she was ready to go on a date. That way she kept romance alive. My dad always thought she was the best and most beautiful.

My father was not as outgoing as my mom. He got along with and enjoyed other people when they were around, yet he liked to come home after work and usually stayed there unless there was something special going on. He was an avid reader and there were few days he didn't read well into the night. He had a slight heart defect and his mother never let him roughhouse when he was growing up so he read a lot from then on. My dad's grandfather was a Lutheran minister—I think first generation from Germany. He died when my paternal grandfather was thirteen years old. That meant that granddad had to quit school and work to support the rest of the family since he was the oldest. He was always a great advocate of education, but my dad was the only one of his four children to get a college degree. My dad loved the woods and trees and his degree was in Forestry. He and my mom had a great love of nature which was passed on to my sister and me.

My paternal grandfather was quite an entrepreneur, in spite of his early years and lack of education. He managed to buy a grocery store and then a dry cleaning plant in Pittsburgh, Pennsylvania. During the depression he went bankrupt and lost the dry cleaning business. He managed, however, to go to Florida and buy acres of orange groves and also 160 acres of apple and peach orchards and beautiful wooded land near Gettysburg (Pa.). The "Farm" as they called the Gettysburg land had a house built during the Civil War. It had hand-hewn oak floors, rafters, and staircase, and granddad built a fieldstone fireplace the length of the living room. We would roast chestnuts and marshmallows in the coals on cool nights. My grandfather also added a screen porch and a very large country kitchen, big enough to seat the whole family. My grandmother cooked the best smothered fried chicken in the world.

When I was about eight years old my grandparents built a log cabin in the woods for family to stay when they came to visit for a while. They had also made a picnic ground down in the south woods with a beautiful clear stream running through it, complete with tables and benches and another fieldstone fireplace. Granddad always planted one whole field of corn just for family, and we would have corn roasts when it was ready for picking. No other corn has ever tasted so good!!! There was also a part of the apple crop that was made into cider and saved until it was just a tad hard. How I loved it!! One time, granddad had a keg of it in the front yard with a rubber tube to siphon it up. He told me I could have some, and it just kept running faster than I could swallow it, and it ran into the ground. What a waste!!! Oh yum!!!! Then when the peaches were ripe, he and my grandmother would get out the ice cream freezer and make fresh peach ice cream. For supper we would have only huge bowls smothered with slices of juicy, fresh peaches. They were the best!! Probably five inches in diameter and so juicy the juice would run down your arms when you took a bite. It always seemed that when we had that meal it would take forever for the ice cream to freeze.

My grandmother looked just like a grandma should look. She always met my sister and my cousins and me with a cookie jar full of fresh baked cookies, just like a grandma should. I can never remember either of my grandparents raising their voices to any of us, although I'm sure we must have deserved it once in a while anyway. I remember one time my cousin Nancy and I were down near the barn and we heard this rattling sound from a ditch that was overgrown with weeds. We couldn't figure out what it was and we decided it must be a rattlesnake shaking its rattles. We became very frightened at that point and took off running for the house. We told my grandparents and they came out to the ditch, with us following behind. What they found was a rabbit with its foot caught in a heavy steel trap, trying to drag it along. Its foot was cut through to the bone, and it was too slow to get away from us. Granddad picked it up and my grandmother held it down while he amputated the foot and bandaged it up. I will never forget that rabbit. It laid there like it knew we were trying to help it, and then it got up and hopped away. Granddad told my cousin and me he saw that three legged rabbit when he was in the woods one day, but he may have told us that just to make us feel good!!!

My grandma loved flowers, and her flower garden at the farm ran the full length of the yard. It must have been 70 feet long and 10 feet wide. She had every kind of flower imaginable, and every color, yet I don't remember her working in it. Life seemed much simpler then, but perhaps that is just a child's view.

My nuclear family spent many summers there at the cabin. We slept out on a big screened porch on cots, listening to the whippoorwills at night. My mom and my sister and I would be there all summer and dad would come for the weekend after he finished work on Fridays. We all played mandolins and would often play together, and I would sing. No one else in the family could stay on key. We would all go to Gettysburg on Saturdays to get groceries and take a picnic lunch. After we shopped we would go out to the Gettysburg Battlefield and have our picnic at either Spangler's Spring or Devil's Den. I grew up loving stories about the Civil War era. They were romantic and didn't describe the carnage that took place; at least not in children's books.

We had plenty of time to relax, read, and be outdoors during those summers on the farm. My sister used to take our hound dog, Duke, and go hiking in the woods. Unless there was an adult along, I usually opted for staying closer to civilization. I would go with her when we went to the picnic grounds where there was a large clearing. We would work for days, sometimes damming up the creek and swimming in the swimming hole we had just completed. We would also spend days building villages out of moss, sticks, and rocks, and populating them with flower people. It was always cool in the woods by the stream even when it was hot in the houses. My grandparents had built a swimming pool at the south end of the apple orchards, where I learned to swim when I was two years old, but by the time Marcia and I were creating dams, the pool had fallen into disrepair and was good for nothing beyond catching tadpoles and frogs.

My dad went to work for the Civil Conservation Corp (CCC) when I was two or three years old. It had come into being shortly after the great depression, or maybe even during it, to provide unemployed young men jobs and education. Being a Forester, this was right up his alley. He was a Supervisor at camps in Tennessee, Maryland, and Pennsylvania. He had some "hairy" stories to tell about Tennessee, about coming across moonshine operations back in the Appalachian Mountains. They were illegal, and it was dangerous to find them because it was a productive business and the moonshiners would shoot you if they felt threatened.

Dad loved being in the woods and was pleased with the reforestation projects they were creating. I used to love going for hikes in the woods with my dad. He would teach me about the different trees and their leaves, and how to tell how old they were. He also liked to tell me the Latin names and he got a kick out of my pronunciations. I loved feeling him hold my little hand in his big hand. It always made me feel loved and safe.

In those early summers of my life, my parents ran an inn for the CCC in a little summer resort called Pine Grove Furnace (which I mentioned earlier). It was about twelve miles from Carlisle, Pennsylvania. The Appalachian Mountains run right near Pine Grove and it is some of the most beautiful country I've ever seen. It is similar to some of the mountainous country in North Carolina. It made an unforgettable impression on me even as a three and four year old. I can still visualize the clear streams tumbling over huge rocks with woods filled with rhododendrons and other plants and trees.

Pine Grove had a lake that had been an iron ore mine during the Revolutionary War when it was illegal to mine the ore and turn it into weapons against the British. The old furnace was still standing, but, as you might imagine, it was quite dilapidated. You could still find slag with beautiful shades of blue and green lying around on the ground. The ore hole had filled up with spring water and it was very deep and very cold even in midsummer. We spent most of our days swimming. My fondest daydream was being a mermaid and never having to leave the water.

My family loved nature and the woods, as I mentioned earlier. We enjoyed the animals that were abundant in that part of the country. I, however, was terrified of snakes, which were also plentiful in the forests of Pennsylvania. There was a mountain man who would come to the inn every once in a while and he always had a burlap sack full of rattlesnakes. He, and whatever men were around at the time, would put the snakes in a cardboard box and stand back and tease the snakes with long sticks to provoke them into striking. My dad would usually be with the other men, and I would be terrified that he would be bitten. Mom also worried that Marcia and I might be snake bitten and coached us often on how we should behave if we came across a copperhead or rattler. She got her message across loud and clear because I was always afraid if I couldn't see the area ahead of me to know it was safe.

My sister Marcia, however, was another story. She didn't have the fears that I did, ever. The Game Warden lived next door to the Inn in Pine Grove Furnace, and he collected venom from rattlesnakes to make anti-venom. My sister would hold the rattlers' mouths open for him to milk the fangs to collect the poison. I was always so terrified for her that it would make me almost physically sick when she did it. My parents must have felt that the warden had control of the situation, because they allowed her to do it. I, personally, would have died right there on the spot rather than touch one of the reptiles. Marcia was a born nurse and went to Nursing School when I was twelve years old. I have always believed that nurses are born and not made. I was sure about that with my sister.

Once when Marcia was a teenager, we were walking down a country road and a car came along. Just as it got almost even with us, a rabbit jumped out in front of it and was run over. The car never stopped. The rabbit wasn't dead however, but almost so, and it was flopping around on the road while I stood there with my insides all scrunched together. Marcia calmly walked over to where it was, picked it up, and gave it a karate chop to the neck, killing it instantly. She couldn't bear to see it in pain and was able to end it. I couldn't bear to see it in pain either, but there was no way I could do what she did. I thought my big sister was amazing and I came close to worshipping her. She was one of those people who could walk into a room if you were sick, and you instantly felt better. Another fearless action of hers, when she was hiking in the woods with Duke, was to somehow build a ring of stones around a copperhead snake and trap it. Then she came back to the farm and got dad and granddad, and they went back and shot it. I think perhaps we would not do that today, but at that time that's what we did. The only time I went into the woods by myself, I couldn't get the full benefit of its beauty because I was too apprehensive. Only as I have gotten much older have I lost that fear.

I had an early grounding experience which has stuck with me all my life. There was a big camping ground near the lake in Pine Grove with an earth track where feet had worn the grass away. The dirt was packed down very hard and dark brown in color. It seemed, when I was small, that it was a long way around, and we walked around it quite often. There was one particular spot that I loved because it was so smooth and it felt like velvet to my feet. I liked to go to that place and rub my bare foot over it again and again.

During these growing up years, I had a few traumatic experiences that affected my life deeply. The first one I remember happened when I was two years old. My mother became ill with hepatitis. She was, of course, quarantined and I wasn't allowed to see her. At one point in her illness, she must have thought she might not live because she had someone bring me to the door of her room so she could see me. I remember seeing her and being aware of how yellow her skin was. This image stuck in my mind clearly. I even later described which room at the Inn she was in, and where each piece of furniture was placed. (Experiences like this at very young ages are often clearly remembered, as I found out from many clients in psychotherapy when I was a Clinical Social Worker). I must have felt abandoned by my mom during that time she was ill because I have had so many abandonment issues, but not only with my mom.

When I was in first or second grade, dad was a Forester in a little town called Indian Head, Maryland, and he disappeared for about six weeks. This was very unusual for my dad as he was generally thoughtful and caring. My mom was very distraught, although she must have learned from his supervisor where he was because he didn't lose his job. He had gone to Walter Reed Hospital for knee surgery. I can't even imagine why he did such a thing. Mom was able to carry on at home, although I think it hurt her badly and she was probably very angry with him. There are many things I would like to know that I didn't dare to ask about when my parents were living.

The greatest trauma of my life, however, was caused by a man who came to work for my parents at the Inn in Pine Grove in the summers. He did handyman work around the place. He also played a guitar and taught me many songs, and I followed him around like a puppy dog. I adored him and I thought he loved me. He had been working for my parents for several summers and they trusted him implicitly. He sexually abused me the summer I was six years old and told me he would kill me if I told what he had done. I believed him!!!!

Three little girls were murdered that same summer and left on a blanket in the woods thirteen miles from Pine Grove Furnace, very near Carlisle. It was nationally known as the "Babes in the Woods" murder. It happened so close to Pine Grove that the Inn became the center for the investigation where all the detectives and others involved gathered to discuss the case.

I heard the men talking about it and I have a visual impression of seeing a lot of legs. I must have been sitting on the floor, out of the way, listening. Glossy photos were left on the table and, of course, I looked at them when no one was around. The children were laying face-up on a blanket surrounded by woods. They had scratches on their faces, arms, and legs; otherwise they looked as though they were sleeping. There were no other obvious signs that they were dead. I thought for sure that our handyman was the murderer. He may have implied that to me to frighten me (and did). I connected the two events and the results were terrifying.

I never knew of any closure on the murder until years later when I looked it up in old newspaper files. I found out that the father of the children and a woman who was thought to be a cousin of the father, were found dead in a bus station. They were in a town that was located fairly close to where the girls were found. It was thought that the couple was despondent because of their financial situation. Information gathered about the family showed that they had been moving around from place to place and working when they could find temporary employment. The authorities believed the couple had killed the girls in desperation and then committed suicide. However, I continued to believe our handyman had done it.

I had all the classic symptoms of sexual abuse. I had so many different emotions and, of course, no frame of reference. I had feelings of unreality; this couldn't be happening to me. I couldn't believe this man who was so good to me could possibly harm me. I had thought he truly adored me. On the other hand I felt tremendous rage and debilitating fear. At the same time I felt sadness and loss, and I had the sense that I had lost my "goodness" because I wanted him to go away and even die. My body felt dirty and I was shamed by what he had done.

He sometimes chopped firewood and would look at me in a threatening way when he brought the axe down on the wood. One time the axe flew off the handle and cut his shoulder, and I was glad and felt relieved for awhile. I never did tell anyone about what happened to me because I was too terrified.

It took me a long time to behave normally. I had always gotten along well with other children, and I didn't for two or three years. I felt they didn't like me, and I hated some of them. I felt terribly insecure. I despised my second grade teacher with a passion. I don't think she was a particularly warm person but she didn't deserve my displaced rage. Of that much I am sure. By that time I didn't realize where all these feelings had come from. I just knew I was horrendously unhappy and I didn't know why or how to cope with the emotions. I did, however, find a way to help me survive. I didn't do it consciously, but I visualized a little black tin box of the type that was used in those days. It had a lid that fit down inside, so it didn't open easily. A bit of the paint was scraped off so that the bare metal shone through. I put all of my pain in that little black box and as the years went by I would sometimes carefully lift a corner of the lid in my psyche, and the pain would come roaring out. I would quickly push it back inside and slam the top back down. I knew it was there but I didn't deal with it until I became an adult.

Gradually, I began to think that I had just imagined the abuse and didn't believe it had actually happened. My fourth grade teacher really liked me and was helpful to me, giving me extra responsibilities and support until I finally started to come out of the slump I was in. It was as though she sensed that I was troubled and reached out to me. I'm sure my parents must have noticed the changes in me, but I don't believe they ever questioned me and I don't believe they ever figured it out. In the second grade two boys took my books away from me on the way home from school and threw them down a sewer. They told me they would kill me if I told. As before, I never told, even though I was punished for "losing" the books.

Later, as an adult when my marriage was breaking up, I started talking about what I thought I remembered in group therapy. All of a sudden it was like the floodgates of hell opened up before me and there was Armageddon! It was so excruciatingly painful that once again I shut the gates as quickly as possible. I knew then it was real, however, and I would have to deal with it and somehow heal if I wanted to be whole. And I did! A little at a time I started working on the issues so that it was bearable. It took me a long time and the major part I worked through under hypnosis. Hypnosis is a valuable tool because it allows you to re-experience the traumatic event and at the same time observe it from your reference point as an adult. I have been trained as a hypnotherapist and have used it professionally to help other women resolve similar traumas. I would guess that at least 30% of the women I have had in therapy have been sexually abused as children, usually by someone in their own family. Often I was the first person they had ever told.

There were other lesser traumas in my young life which affected me, but mostly I had a happy childhood with lots of friends and fun activities. My family was generally supportive and caring. We were never yelled at and rarely punished. Home was a comfortable place for us and we were allowed a good deal of freedom within certain boundaries. Our summers were always memorable experiences. One summer I was even allowed to camp out with my sister at the camping grounds at Pine Grove. Marcia was 18 years old then and it must have been right before she went to Nursing School. Mom stayed with friends in a cottage and saw us nearly every day. We did all the cooking and other chores. It was a great experience in independence. My favorite thing to do besides swimming was to take a good book and go to the nearby creek and sit in a hollow of a tree that had fallen across the stream. It was so beautiful and peaceful, and I loved it.

My teenage years were full of new experiences and were sometimes a wonder to me. I was shy and insecure, and I guess it didn't show *too* much. It was a surprise to me that boys sometimes liked me, and I had a couple of fairly long term relationships during high school. I had some short ones in between and sometimes I didn't have any. My parents bought an old cottage on Lake Erie which could easily sleep twelve people. It was a wonderful old place, where you could open up the big shutters on the bedroom windows and listen to the sounds of the waves slapping against the shore. My girlfriends were always welcome, and usually a crowd of them were there with me.

Dad loved to tease us girls and wake us up in the mornings by dripping drops of cold water on our faces to make us squeal. Once in a while our boyfriends were allowed to spend the night. Some of the girls would double up, but mostly there were enough rooms for everyone. Mom would get up early and fix a humongous breakfast of pancakes and bacon. As I am writing this book I am feeling greater appreciation for my parents and grandparents than I ever have before. How blessed I was. We didn't have much money. Mom had a few stocks that had been willed to her and with the little bit they got from that, they were able to do some extraordinary things to make life better and more fun for me (my sister was away from home by then).

A girl by the name of Tudy Loomis was my best friend in high school. She came from an operatic family and had a gorgeous voice. I liked to sing and so did the rest of my crowd. After we were all worn out from swimming, beaching, and boating we would sit around for hours, singing the popular songs of the time. Tudy was always there to lead us and keep us on key. We were not the "fast crowd" at school. None of us drank alcohol, and there were no drugs available. I doubt if any of us would have done them if there had been anyway. Times were different in that generation before TV's, cell phones, or ipods. I also liked to dance and went to a lot of dances, both ballroom and square. I found most school classes boring, but got decent grades and loved the social activities.

16

My dad had come to Florida during my senior year in high school, to help my grandparents in the fruit shipping business. They were getting older, and it was becoming too difficult for them to handle it alone. My mom and I stayed in an upstairs apartment in my friend Tudy's home so that I wouldn't have to change schools in my final year. I didn't want to go to college, at least not right away, and I was more interested in art school. I hated moving and leaving friends, but I was looking forward to getting through school and creating a new life.

At this point I want to say something about my spiritual growth and evolution while I was growing up. My mother always went to church and was involved in its activities. We belonged to the Methodist church most of the time, but not always. Whenever we moved to a new town, (which was often as I was growing up, twelve schools in twelve years and nearly as many churches) mom would visit several parishes before choosing one we would attend. If there was a lot of hellfire and brimstone preached in a sermon we wouldn't go there. We would go to the place that was more moderate in their beliefs. Consequently, I never felt that I had to believe in any one particular dogma or religious creed. I really felt free to choose what I could accept. I always knew, without a doubt, that God was a loving God. I remember wanting to impress that fact on some of the kids in my Sunday School class when the class was defining the nature of God. Even in the years I was so traumatized I knew that God was love.

My first memories of church were of Pine Grove, where there was a little nondenominational church tucked in at the edge of a woods. It had a sanctuary, but that was all. Sunday school classes were held outdoors in natural settings. Everyone would meet together in the sanctuary first and sing hymns. I loved to sing and I would stand up on the pew so that I could see, and I would sing at the top of my lungs. I know almost all the first verses and when we got to the second or third verse I continued to sing just as loudly without words. I loved it!!

Once when my mom couldn't go, my sister took me to the church service. I went to the front row to sit with some of the other young children. I was probably almost four at the time. The chancel rail right down front had a lovely red velvet cushion on it that was removed for receiving the sacraments. I guess it must have looked too inviting to resist, so I left my seat, climbed up, and turned somersaults on it. I can vaguely remember doing it and embarrassing my sister out of her mind. I think she took me home right away and I was informed that we don't do things like that in church. But I wasn't punished for it. My parents probably thought it was funny.

After the singing when we met for Sunday school, we all had a special spot outside to meet for our own class. The spot for my group was under pine trees at the top of a wooded hill. At the bottom of the hill was a clear mountain stream and woods. Sometimes while we were sitting there, deer would come and drink from the stream. It was an awesome sight and I was struck by the beauty even then. I have no idea what the lessons we heard were about, yet I felt that God was there in that setting. From then on I could always feel God in nature just as much or more than I could in church.

My dad would go with us to church services on special occasions like Christmas and Easter, but he didn't attend regularly. His beliefs were always more metaphysical, although he never talked about his faith or tried to persuade us that he was right. My mom respected his beliefs, but she continued to have hers too. I didn't reject the metaphysical, nor did I wholly accept it either. I was intrigued by reincarnation and kind-of held on to it as a possibility. My dad (as I mentioned before) read a lot, and studied many of the Oriental, Indian, Egyptian, and Persian religions. I'm not positive about the exact nature of his beliefs, but he was a very spiritual person and I have been told by spirit he is on a high spiritual plane.

One day several years ago I had come home from work, and as soon as I opened the front door I was greeted by a strong aroma of some kind of flower I didn't recognize. I couldn't figure out where the scent was coming from, and the fragrance was unlike anything I had noticed before. I kept looking, and finally decided it was coming from my bedroom or the bathroom. But I still couldn't figure out what it was. Later I asked my friend Gordon Banta, a medium and channeler, about what I had experienced. He told me that he saw a man in spirit bringing me spirit flowers. He described my dad in detail. I had quite a few interesting paranormal experiences in that house.

In every church I belonged to I sang in the choir. The music always made me feel closer to God. I know now that it raised my vibrations to a higher level. I have been privileged to sing in some very fine choirs. The first experience that made a tremendous impact on me was during a church camp in Sandusky, Ohio when I was in high school. The leader had been brought in specially, and had a fine reputation throughout the Methodist church. He insisted on commitment and exact attention to his direction. Two hundred young people signed up to be in the choir. What he got out of us musically in a few days time was awe inspiring!! The anthems he had us sing were "How Great Thou Art" and "God So Loved the World". It was the first time I had heard either of them, and I must say that I have never heard them sung more beautifully or with more passion. It was an expansive experience for me. While we were there the war with Germany came to an end.

Later, when my children were little, we belonged to a small Methodist church. The choir was led by a woman who had great feelings and excellent musical skills. There was a special feeling of cohesiveness in that congregation. The pastor was the first that I knew who talked about the "unconditional" quality of God's love. One day I was sitting in a pew and he lightly touched me on the top of my head as he walked past. Quickly the thought went through my mind, "don't say that unless you really mean it". Of course he really didn't "say" anything but I felt the message. I felt the vibration from the top of my head to the soles of my feet. I had never felt that kind of loving energy before. I am sure that all of us in that church experienced an inclusiveness few of us had felt before. The choir had a wonderful élan that made our music extra fine.

Wanting to learn who I really was, I did a great deal of reading and studying of spiritual materials when I was in my early thirties, and I came across an article in the Saturday Evening Post, part of a series called "Adventures of the Mind". The article was by Paul Tillich, a famous theologian, who envisioned God as the "Ultimate Concern". I was rather startled by what this article had to say. It was unusual for me to react that way, and I can't remember what it said that caused me to respond in such an unusual manner. I also don't recall thinking much more about the article over a period of time. The strange thing about it was that perhaps ten years later, I ran across it again. I reread it to see what it was that had caused me to have such a strong reaction before, and for the life of me I couldn't see one thing that didn't already fit into my belief system! It appeared that I had unconsciously adopted Tillich's pathway and wasn't even aware of what I had done.

Since then, I have become metaphysical, still believing in the sacred or divine consciousness, and I had a dream which I will share with you. I dreamed that someone in my family was pregnant and that Christ was visiting in our home. The atmosphere felt very comfortable and warm. Jesus was instructing us how to prepare to deliver the baby via C-Section. It seemed a very natural situation. My interpretation is that it was about Christ consciousness being "birthed" into the world (my family). I had another dream during the time I was attending Gordon Banta's psychic spiritual classes. In this dream, I had a picture of the Mother Mary hanging on my wall and she started talking to me from the picture. But I couldn't understand what she was saying to me. The following night, in Gordon's class while he was channeling, Mary came through. I asked her what she had been saying to me in the dream and she told me that she would be at Gordon's house the next night. She then went on to tell us things about the life of Christ that are not commonly known. So much has happened to me since that time. It is impossible to do more than skim the surface.

All during these years I was searching and working on myself to reach a place of eternal JOYFULLNESS. I must say, however, that I didn't know there was a place that you could always feel or "tap" into your JOY. I didn't know it until I got there. It was elusive for a long time, yet it was only a few years before I had my breakthrough. I know that my experiences with Gordon Banta were a gift that was like a final bridge to the environment where I would find the core of my being which is always unconditional love and everlasting JOY!!!!

After I graduated from high school, mom and I moved from Ohio to Florida to join my dad. We lived in Orlando before Disney, Epcot, or Sea World. Everything exploded after they came into being. When we first lived there it was a nice quiet town. Shortly after we moved there I started going to the Vocational School where I studied Commercial Art The instructor was an Englishman who actually did "fine art". He worked almost totally in pen and ink and had been commissioned by the Royal English Family to do the art work for their fine china. He did beautiful work and I learned a great deal. I became proficient in capturing the likenesses of models. I have lost the ability to get an accurate likeness in a short amount of time because I didn't continue to practice eight hours a day.

I met my future husband at that school. He was studying Drafting and we soon started dating. My parents wanted me to go to Ringling Art School in Sarasota and I too wanted to go there. I hated going away from Ed, who was working by then, yet I could go home on weekends and Ed could come visit me. I went in the fall and it was both a happy and unhappy experience for me. I thought I was a fairly talented artist; but soon I began to wonder if I was any good at all. The instructors had me doing things in an entirely different manner than I was used to and I didn't like the way my work looked. Besides, I was really homesick for Ed. We had been going together for more than a year and had pretty much decided that we would get married. I was feeling quite insecure. After a semester I decided not to go back to Ringling and went ahead with wedding plans.

My first child was born after a year, a beautiful little boy with titian blonde curls. He was a bright child who started triggering my hang-ups when he reached the age of two and started saying "no". I recognized that I had some of the same immature emotions in myself, and that I didn't like them, yet I didn't know what to do about them in either of us. I just wanted to get rid of the anger, the guilt, and the control issues, but they didn't just go away because I wanted them to; and so I struggled. I didn't think to look for books on child discipline but I tried to be more cognizant of what I was doing.

My mom and I had disagreements because she thought I was wrong at times and I know I did make lots of mistakes. I remember one instance when Ed was about five and I took him to buy something for his dad as a birthday present. I tried to guide him to a section of items that I thought his dad would like, but he was insistent on buying something that he himself liked. I don't remember what it was, yet it wasn't a toy; it was some sort of figurine or something like that. Mom thought that I should "make" him get a gift that was more appropriate. I allowed him to get what he wanted and that was fine with Ed, although he didn't make much of a fuss over it. This was one of the first times I really stood up to my mom and didn't let her control me.

When my son Ed was two, my husband Ed and I decided we wanted another baby, and I quickly became pregnant again. Around the seventh month, I started having problems and ended up having a toxic pregnancy. I felt like there were a hundred hammers pounding in my head and ended up in the hospital heavily sedated, while the doctors tried to bring my blood pressure under control. The first few days were vague as I would wake up, throw up, and then go right back to sleep. I heard or knew that I had pre-eclampsia, but not much else. They finally woke me up and told me they wanted to do a C-section because nothing was working well and I could go into convulsions and die. I remember signing the papers for surgery but not being able to see the line I was to sign on because my vision was so blurry. I was also full of fluid and there were no diuretics yet.

21

I wanted to be awake when they cut me open so that I could see that the baby was all right. I felt the pressure of the scalpel as they made the incision and I heard the baby make a little mewling sound. They said it was a little girl and then I went to sleep. Dr. Crews, who was my doctor, told me not to get my hopes up because my baby was only two pounds and three ounces and had only a ten percent chance of survival.

There were no neonatal units back then, and the baby was also toxic from me. Hope is a strong factor, however, and I couldn't help but hope. I told the Dr. that no matter what happened, I wanted to see my baby. I felt that if she didn't make it, I needed to know who I was grieving for. I don't remember how long she lived but it was several hours. When Ed and my mother walked in the room after that, they didn't have to tell me, I knew. My maternal grandmother had died when I was young, and that had been the only significant death in my life up to that point.

I was twenty-three years old and totally unprepared for the devastation I felt. The baby was brought in to me and I touched her but I was afraid if I held her I would never be able to let her go. My mother was there with me, but Ed was exhausted as he had lived at the hospital for all the days I had been there. One lock of his hair turned completely white during that week. The time that my baby was brought to me was like a little island out of time that I shall never forget. The first night after the baby died, it stormed and the wind whipped the palm fronds on the palms around the hospital. I thought at the time that I would never hear that sound ever again without my heart breaking.

There was little talk of death in the 50's and not much, if any, grief literature. The nurses would stop me if I started to cry in the hospital, so I had to wait until I got home. I knew without question that healing would come from doing the daily chores, like sweeping the floors, making the beds, and caring for my small son who was profoundly affected by my being away from him. He was afraid for me to be out of his sight. If I went somewhere without him he would grab my clothing and hold on as tightly as possible. I would have to pry his hands away and reassure him that I would be back. At bedtime, I would sit with him until he fell asleep or he would stay awake all night. This went on for about a year. I didn't know then that young children become depressed when their major caregiver is gone (for whatever reason) for as little as three days. I was hospitalized for ten. During that time my sister-in-law took care of him. He said to her one day after going through her sewing machine drawers and finding a button, "If I swallow this button, you'll have to take me to the hospital where my mommy is, won't you?" It was a difficult time for him and it affected his ability to trust the most important person in his life.

When I was discharged from the hospital, everything looked different to me. It was as if every leaf on every tree stood out individually, and with a clarity I had never witnessed before. I also felt totally opened up, and my emotions were at a peak. I was able to feel the love people I hardly even knew were showing to me. So there were good things that came out of my grief. I felt a lot of support and I don't remember any of the hurtful things people sometimes say when they're trying to help yet don't know how, such as, "You can have another baby later." My grief lasted for a long time. I wasn't able to ask Ed about the funeral for the baby for about two years because it was so painful.

Something else began during those months of grief. I began asking myself eternal questions: "Why am I here? Am I just supposed to be a wife and mother, or do I have another purpose for being on this earth?" My values, which had been pretty fair anyway, began to change to more spiritual values and I realized that nothing was very important except love. I saw that when everything was put into perspective, love was everything. My mind was racing, going 150 miles an hour it felt like. The self-searching I did was a fairly long process, maybe several months or a year or even more. Then finally it came to me that I was to be a "channel for God's love", in just exactly those words.

I didn't know the term channeling as we use it today. I didn't know how to love without condition (at least I didn't think I knew). I don't think I was really even familiar with "unconditional love", although I believed God's love to be without condition. I just didn't call it that. I decided I would learn to love as much like God as was humanly possible, and I made tons of mistakes along the way and suffered much emotional pain.

I had pushed almost all angry feelings away into my subconscious, as it was not acceptable for little girls to express anger in any direct way. I remember one time when I was four that I had done something to displease my mother. She got a willow switch and switched me from my ankles up to my bottom, leaving red welts up and down my legs. I was so furious I wanted to kill her. I knew that whatever I had done I didn't deserve that, but I didn't cry. Instead I told her "that didn't hurt." From then on, she never spanked me again but used guilt, which hurt much

23

worse. Whenever she was unhappy with me she would tell me that I hurt her or my dad. I learned to be sneaky and to go "underground" and to rarely get caught.

As I started to grow emotionally in earnest, I discovered that there was a part of me that wanted to remain unhealthy. We call it "resistance" in the psychological field, but I didn't know it then. I decided to see if I could conquer it, so I jumped in my car and drove to Hillsborough State Park, just north of Tampa. It was a pleasant day and I sat at a concrete picnic table on a concrete bench and I went back and forth in what felt like emotional arm wrestling for two or three hours. When I was done, I knew that I had won. I knew without a doubt that the healthy part of me would never give up. Because of that experience, I made a commitment to myself that I would continue to grow to be as whole and aware as it is humanly possible. There were times I got very tired, especially in those first few years, but I kept on. Eventually it did get better and better and better.

After we lost our little girl, Ed and I waited a few years and had another son who was just as easy as the first son had been a challenge. When he was two we moved to Tampa and I did a lot of searching through books and articles to help myself grow. Ed didn't want me to work and be away from the children. We bought a boat and did a lot of water skiing and playing on the weekends, and involved ourselves in many church activities. Ed had a good job and traveled during the week. It worked out beautifully. He was gone Monday through Thursday and when he got home on Fridays we were all glad to see him. The weekends were full with skiing and picnics, friends and church, and the time flew by. I also became more independent and found children easier to handle by myself during the week.

I was growing emotionally and Ed wasn't. He was about the same, and it worked okay until he stopped traveling and was home every night. He started being unhappy about my extracurricular activities which took maybe two nights a week. Thinking I would please him I stopped everything but choir practice. Guess what? It didn't make any difference. It was as though I hadn't changed anything. He still complained as much as usual. I know now that that it was his inability to control me which he was picking up loud and clear, I just didn't recognize it then.

Our marriage started to fall apart, and where I had felt I was on solid ground emotionally the sand started shifting beneath my feet. I was angry and couldn't admit it to myself, and I was doing a lot of blaming, which got me nowhere. I started feeling terrible anxiety. It was as if I were "blowing in the wind". I didn't know who I was and it was surely hell. I felt so insecure I was miserable. I started going to therapy, and over time I became more or less comfortable most of the time. I tried to get Ed to go with me but he refused, and he eventually published a notice in the newspaper that he would no longer be responsible for my counseling bills. That killed all the feelings I had left for him. Before that I had another little girl whom I wanted very much. I felt my family was finally complete with her birth, and yet it was falling apart.

The University of South Florida opened for the first time in the fall of 1961, about seven miles from my house. I went to a luncheon where one of the Deans spoke, and I knew I had to get my degree. Ed didn't want me to enroll, but I got the money from my parents and signed up for one course. Ed was furious with me yet I went anyway. I tried to get him to attend, as he had wanted to get a college education when he was discharged from the army. His father had died a year before that and his mother talked him out of going and leaving her. He had started his own Air Conditioning business by then and could have easily taken the time and the money, but he refused. I continued to take courses, yet I felt I had to be devious because Ed never changed his attitude about my going. I would ask his bookkeeper at his business for tuition and she would always give it to me. He would never reprimand her since he did not want to lose face with her. And he wouldn't say anything to me about it, yet I knew he hated it. Eventually the marriage ended. Maybe it wouldn't have had I handled issues differently, though I doubt it would have made much difference. I was on a mission, and that changed everything.

After our divorce I borrowed money from our bank to continue my education. I was fortunate because women in the 60's rarely succeeded in setting up credit. I had been turned down when I tried to buy a push lawn mower, based on the fact that I had no credit. Ed and I had had a bank loan, so I went to the bank president and told him I needed funds to continue my education. He asked me, "How much do you need?" I nearly fell off my seat. I remember that I told him one hundred and fifty dollars. Can you imagine going to a university for anything for that amount of money today? Later I got student loans, but I knew I would be able to get another loan from my bank if I really needed additional money for my education.

It was a real struggle those years in school. Ed was so angry with me that he wanted to get even by not paying child support. I was determined he would pay, as I didn't want to work a regular job and go to school at the same time. I knew some women who did, and they were never home with their kids. I couldn't do that to my three children who were ages one, five, and nine when I first started. As a result of my determination I was in court twelve times in twenty-four months. The judge would order Ed to pay and he wouldn't, so back we'd go. I finally found an attorney who was willing to threaten him with permanent contempt of court and he spent one weekend in jail when he didn't pay up, and that was the end of that. From then on he paid. The money still wasn't great, even with the child support, so I took a job for ten hours a week as a student assistant. The hours were flexible so I could schedule my classes and work while the kids were in school and nursery school. The job paid a dollar an hour. Not much but $1.00 went a lot further than it does today. One summer I took a break and worked in a department store. After I paid the babysitter there was almost nothing left. The company wanted to make me a buyer but that didn't fit with my plans, so I turned it down and went back to college in the fall.

I don't know how I managed to survive those years. I think it was only pure grit that got me through. You could have run over me with a steam roller and I would have gotten right back up and gone on. I rarely studied until I got the children in bed, and then I would read and do whatever was necessary until the wee hours of the morning. Once I'd get the kids to their different schools I would oftentimes pull into the university parking lot and sleep for fifteen minutes before class.

It took me five years to graduate yet I had some good times along the way. It wasn't all work and no play!!! I had a good friend, Jane, who lived close to me and who was an English/speech major. About the same time I was going through my divorce, her husband had a brain tumor and went into a coma. Mike had been in business for himself and had let the family insurance and hospitalization lapse because of his mental state. As luck would have it, Jane only found out after the fact. Mike was in Tampa General Hospital for quite a while and never became conscious again. The hospital asked Jane to move him to a nursing home, and his dad threatened to kill Jane if she did. Things were quite "hairy" for a while. Finally she had no choice, and the dad was able to accept that Mike was not going to get well. He lived in that state for over a year before he died. During that time Jane and I were able to give each other a lot of mutual support. After Mike died and my divorce was final we did have many good times together.

I remember one experience in particular that was really unusual. Jane, my friend, was dog sitting for some friends while they went on vacation. Their home was on a lake and Jane invited me to come out and spend the weekend and swim and have some fun. Jane had her wirehaired terrier, Reggie, with her, and as soon as I got there she told me he was behaving strangely. Every morning Reggie would want to go out the very first thing and would head straight for the lake. He would pace back and forth along the shore for hours at a time. He would do this all day long, and when Jane would call him he wouldn't come to her as usual and, in fact, didn't even seem to hear her. To get him to come in to the house she would have to go and bodily lift him out of the water. He would be tired trembling all over. If she let him loose outside, he would head straight back to the lake. She thought maybe he had gotten engrossed in watching minnows or small fish, and she wanted me to see if I could figure out what was going on. There were no fish or other creatures but I could see as I watched him that he was looking at *something*. I finally realized he was watching reflections on the water and this was hypnotizing him. That was why he didn't hear her when she called him. He was one little exhausted doggy. We had a good laugh about that and Jane made sure he stayed in the house after that for the rest of their stay there.

During my junior and senior years at USF I was doing some volunteer work at the County Hospital Psychiatric unit and I was also observing group therapy on a weekly basis with a local psychiatrist. My goal was always to go into the Mental Health field and I wanted to be as well prepared as possible. I was always looking for avenues of opportunity to learn everything that could be helpful to me and to grow personally.

The University decided to have their first overseas study program in Mexico the summer of 1965. One of my professors had been going to Guatemala each year and doing a literacy program in a small village. He had a slide show of life as it was for the villagers and he showed it to those of us who might be interested in the overseas study. When I saw the slides I knew I had to go if there was any way possible. I chose as my study the Mental Health System of Mexico, having no idea if they even had one. As part of my preparation I wrote a letter to the Mexican government asking for information and telling them about my plans. I didn't hear from them, but I went anyway, taking my middle son Chip with me and leaving my oldest son with his dad. My daughter Marcia went to Oregon with my mother to visit my sister Marcia.

As a result of the letter I had sent to the government and some faux pas, I was treated royally and given an office in a beautiful new teaching hospital. A Mexican psychiatrist trained in the United States was appointed my mentor, and I was given access to the Presidential files regarding mental health, translators at every facility I visited, and usually most of a whole day's tour and presentation of their program. They even sent a van to pick me up at our apartment and transport me to the facilities and back again. I later found out they had never had anyone from the United States to see what they were doing.

I was very impressed with the sophistication of their programs. They had a broader range of services than we did in Florida, and were continually trying to upgrade and get people out into the community as much as possible. The oldest mental hospital in the western hemisphere is in Mexico City, or it was at that time. The government was building new facilities to house the psychotic or mentally challenged and dementia patients. One huge difference with the Mexican population was that there was a strong stigma against mental illness and retardation, or any of the disorders of that nature. Families from all over the country would bring the afflicted to the old hospital and leave them on the door step, and the family would disappear, forever.

As fast as the new facilities would be built and people placed in them from the hospital, it would fill up again with more people The unfortunate result was that the more functional individuals were sent to the newer programs, and the hospital was left filled with badly dysfunctional persons. The aides who took care of the patients were so poor that they would steal the few clothes the patients had when they came or were given to them by the hospital. It was not at all unusual to see patients with only a sheet or blanket wrapped around their bodies. The day I was there the food for lunch was a thin gruel type soup with chunks of bread.

The children's area was astounding. Many of the children were naked (and it was cold). One little boy was jaundiced and not separated from the others who were being hosed down with cold water in a courtyard. Some of them had feces in their hair. Other children who were profoundly retarded were tied to beds on bare mattresses. I was told that sometimes at night the rats ran over the beds and children.

There was a Quaker lady from the United States who was volunteering two or three days a week at that hospital and trying to get conditions changed. It was very sad. I was appalled and I could tell you much more, but I won't do that here.

Other programs like their granjas (farms) were a wonderful idea where people received training in various vocations such as shoe repair. Others went to functional farms in the area and worked during the day, then would come back to their own granja at night. On weekends spouses could come and stay overnight if they chose to do so.

My son Chip chose to go with me to Mexico where he fell in love with mangos, and when I got lost, which was often in Mexico City, it was usually Chip who got me going in the right direction. It seemed to me that being away from my own culture and being totally on my own was growth-producing for me. I was with one other student in the apartment we rented, although there were other people from the university in Mexico City if we needed them. We had some very interesting experiences and met some fantastic people. It was altogether a very heartwarming trip and I was gradually becoming more accepting (yet not embracing) of myself, and much more independent.

After I graduated from USF (as a member of their charter class), I started looking around for a job with the potential for learning about the mental health field. I finally found exactly what I wanted through a woman I knew from a group I belonged to. She was in the Social Services Department of Polk County Hospital. I really wasn't interested in Social Services so I finally made an appointment with the Human Resources Manager. He was very interested in me because even though I didn't have a masters degree I had all the hours of volunteer work plus some therapy for myself.

The hospital decided to open a position for me in the Psychiatric Department. I absolutely loved it!! It is the only job I've ever had where I couldn't wait to get up in the morning to get to work. In the late 1960's there were few laws to protect mentally ill persons. In Florida a family member could go before a judge and sign a petition to have that individual evaluated by a competency committee made up of a psychiatrist and other mental health professionals. Hearings were delayed on the basis of how many persons were waiting for assessment, and how many persons would be seen by the competency committee for how many days a week. After the petition was signed by the judge a police officer was sent to pick up the patient and hold them in jail until the time of their hearing. They were not allowed even one phone call. The " Mental Health Committee" would make a determination of the person's mental status. The patient could then be hospitalized in a local hospital or sent to one of four state mental hospitals, all without due process.

One of my major responsibilities as a Clinical Social Worker was to go to the County jail where patients were held awaiting hearings. Sometimes mentally ill people would be in jail for a month before they were seen by mental health evaluators. I would interview each patient soon after they were put in jail and make a determination if they did indeed have a mental disorder, and if so what that disorder was. I would then make my findings known to the committee on the day the patient had his/her hearing. If the individual was sent to State Hospital, he/she could be kept there until someone decided he was ready to go home. That was sometimes for a very long time, even forever. In the 1970's the Baker Act was passed and it provided legal protections so that patients had representation and couldn't be put away forever without being evaluated every few months.

The psychiatrist that I worked with was a very fine man from Cuba. He had been a doctor in Cuba and also a senator under Battista. When Castro came into power he had led an underground movement to get people out of the country. He left Cuba when Castro found out about his activities and went into Psychiatric residency at Emory University. He ended up at Polk County Hospital where he could work until he got his citizenship. Everyday he would grill me on patient dynamics; and on things like medications. I was already seeing patients for individual and group therapy, and soon he gave me added responsibilities. I learned a great deal about psychiatry and also about myself, and I felt content. I did not, however, feel everlasting joy. Underneath I still felt much insecurity and unworthiness.

I worked at Polk County Hospital for three years and then the administration changed. There was a whole different energy about the place. Dr. Cuervo left because of disagreements with the administrator. I didn't like what I was seeing and hearing, and I started looking around for another job. I wanted to go to graduate school for my Master's degree but I wasn't quite ready at that time.

I decided to take a job with the state of Florida as a Mental Health Representative. I worked out of the Gainesville, Florida Mental Health Clinic, but my boss was the State. My responsibilities covered an area north and west of Gainesville where there had never been any public mental health services—definitely my cup of tea. My job was to see that patients who had been discharged from State Mental facilities got their medications from their local Health Departments and to follow them and give them support to keep them from relapse. I could also develop services in the communities, educate, and do consultation. In effect I could do whatever I felt needed doing. Dr. Stuart Cahoon was acting Director of the clinic and my boss on the local level. He was also a professor of Psychiatry at the University of Florida. He was great and supported me in whatever I wanted to do, which was a lot. The State was planning on starting satellite clinics in the six counties I was in, learning from me what was really "out there". It was a real pioneer job and I had great fun doing it. I started clinics in each county in churches or community agencies or health departments, wherever I could find room. I saw patients referred from any of the court system, agencies, or schools for counseling. I also was instrumental in setting up Mental Health Associations in a few of the counties, and I provided a lot of consultation. I visited schools and found out that children with behavior problems were being put in developmentally challenged classes to give them enough pupils to have the classes. I traveled over 3000 miles a month, and when I went to bed at night I was asleep before my head hit the pillow.

The State was so pleased with what I had done as a Mental Health Rep that when I went to graduate school a year later they opened a field placement for me in the State office. Dr. Stu Cahoon had moved from the Gainesville Clinic and University of Florida to Tallahassee to become the Assistant Director of the Division of Mental Health. I was there just after the Baker Act protecting patient rights was passed, and was privileged to participate in writing the guidelines for it and preparing a presentation for community leaders in preparation of its enactment. I was also allowed to accompany the presenters around the state. It was a truly great experience and I had many good friends on the state level until the state reorganized all the Human Resources and then everything and almost everyone was shuttled someplace else. Everything changes, and that is one law of the universe you can depend on.

One of the most important things that I learned during the early years of my career was that I am responsible for creating my own life. That means every aspect. There are some things we cannot control that have an effect on us, yet we can determine how we think about and respond to issues that are beyond our influence. We are the ones who decide what we think, feel, and focus upon. It took me a while to accept that I really could be in charge of my mind and was fully responsible for changing my thinking to delete as much negative thinking as was humanly possible. This was a huge step. We live in a world that teaches negative thinking and judgment. Like the little sponges that all children are, we soak up negativity and it becomes ingrained and a major part of how we approach life. To change to a more positive thought process is a relearning experience which I will go into more completely, later in this writing.

Underneath my content and ability to function well in my daily life there was still a place where deep pain lived. This pain was so deep for so many years that I couldn't bear to touch into it, much less talk about it. I truly understand that pain and suffering can be so profound that it cannot be acknowledged, or even if it is acknowledged on a personal level, it cannot be shared. I was in my fifties before I found a therapist with whom I felt I could open up the last deep wound.

I had an idea of opening a retirement home based on a holistic model. I had remarried, lived and worked in Texas for a few years, and came back to Florida to be closer to my children. We found a charming building on a lake in a little town outside of Winter Park. It had been built by the railroad baron Henry Flagler and was the first place in Seminole County, Florida, to have electric lights early in the 20th century. There had to be a lot of remodeling done. We did it gradually and started taking people almost immediately. I have lots of good stories and funny ones too, but it would detract from the current narrative. What is relevant is that I had very little illness among my people, and in the six years we had the Inn I had very few deaths or hospitalizations. People tended to stay healthy and happy, and the few that died were healthy until the end when they had a sharp and sudden decline. My program worked very well and the client families were happy because their loved ones were.

I worked closely with client doctors to decrease or discontinue medications that were no longer needed. I talked to many physicians and got to know some of them quite well. Dr. John Tatum was a psychiatrist who was interested in what I was doing at the Inn and the only physician who ever actually visited my facility. I got to know him quite well and decided to see him for therapy. He was as advanced in his own growth as anyone I had ever known. Through him I was introduced to the writing of Brugh Joy who wrote "Joy's Way". John is a fantastic therapist. He has the ability to be confrontational in the most gentle way. I came a very long way with John. I would just like to mention a movie that was helpful to me that came out about the time I was seeing John in 1984. Maybe you will remember it. It was called "Greystoke" and is about the life of Tarzan. There is one scene in it where he finds his ape mother dead, and he lets out a totally haunting cry of horror that can be heard throughout the jungle. To me it is (was) the epitome of the cry of the human spirit in the deepest well of pain. I could feel it as my own. I would recommend it to you if you have this depth of suffering.

"Joy's Way" was an exciting and meaningful book to me. John Tatum had been to his workshops and seminars. He recommended them to me as well as a Vipassanah meditation seminar in the mountains of Massachusetts—a silent ten day retreat where we learned to feel our own vibrations. Energy and vibrational methodologies were just becoming more acceptable in the western hemisphere. Vipassahanah meditation practiced for ten days without any outside stimuli, meaning no verbal or nonverbal contact with other persons, no books, and no writing materials. There was to be nothing distracting from one's inner self and we meditated in a meditation hall for approximately eight hours a day. It was an awesome experience. Even the men and women were separated during all activities. We lived in dormitories in a beautiful old farmhouse and had our own gender related places outdoors to walk and enjoy the countryside. It was an abundant adventure on many levels. I even saw my cat (in spirit form) running along beside me in the fields. I had to have him put to sleep earlier that year as his kidneys failed him. I had been sad for a while, yet when I recognized his spirit I felt such a flowing of joy and there was no way I could feel sad after that experience.

After three days of meditation and mind chattering I began to feel a silence take over and started to feel the first tiny vibrations in my upper lip area. Then in a few more days it felt like every cell in my body was pulsating, and it was. It was extremely exciting and although we were in a sense separated without any of the usual communication, I felt as though I knew people intimately. I was able to pick out every person engaged in a healing profession, which I checked out after we were talking at the end of the seminar. I was right on, and didn't miss anybody. The conclusion of the workshop was a tremendous surprise to me and I believe to everyone there.

We were all in the meditation hall on the day before going home when we were told it was okay to talk. For awhile there was a long period of silence. We were all having different as well as common thoughts: "Do I really want to break this peace?" "How will the others respond to me?" "How will it be talking again?" Finally someone spoke and then everything erupted, and everybody started talking and laughing and it was the highest "high" I've ever known. It was pure JOY!!!! It lasted the whole day with everyone sharing their experiences and all the humorous things that had happened. We laughed a lot and we KNEW each other though none of us had ever met before ten days ago. It was a wonderful and fascinating experience from start to finish. I could not have wished for better.

It was difficult for awhile to be back in ordinary life and time. I could still feel my vibrations whenever I was very still and quiet, but after some weeks I lost that ability, due to daily routines. I was not able to retain the feeling or deep down experience of JOY, and I longed for it. I was searching for avenues that might bring me closer to it, so when I heard about a conference on Brugh Joy's teaching and hands on healing, I knew I had to go.

It was held on the Hawaiian island of Kauai in a large house on a cliff overlooking the ocean. There was a hidden beach 350 feet below the house down a very rugged path. Big pine trees stood along the shoreline with a carpet of pine needles underneath, just made to lie on and watch the waves crash on the shore. All the other attendees knew each other from an earlier conference and the women weren't very friendly. My roommate was very quiet and had little to say to me. The women would congregate in a room at the other end of the house and not tell me anything about it. I felt ostracized. The men befriended me and that felt good yet I missed the close contact with the feminine. I decided not to make an issue of it, but it triggered many abandonment feelings in me and gave me a lot to work on. We met as a group a couple of times a day and as the time went on the women started to warm up to me. By the end of the eleven days most of them were remarking on the clarity of my feelings and were trading addresses with me.

We spent two days during the seminar in silence and fasting. I loved the silent part, although I am not crazy about fasting. I spent most of those two days lying on the cliff on the pine needles meditating and imagining the waves washing over me cleansing all my hurt and traumatic emotions.

Part of our time was spent learning to feel and use energy. I had an advantage, having learned to feel my vibrations at the former workshop. Joy had developed his own method of utilizing universal energy for healing. .It came quite naturally to me and I found out that when I started practicing on someone I would begin to vibrate all over. Over time that has declined but once in a while it still happens. It just means the energy coming through is strong.

Besides practicing with energy on each other, we were provided with opportunities for other activities which were also interesting. Try looking in a mirror for twelve minutes without blinking your eyes. Hard to do, but the results are fascinating. One day we were told to make a musical instrument out of something we found outside in the yard and then perform with it. I don't remember what exactly I made, but I do remember beating on it, so it must have been drum-like. I remember thrumming on it and doing a little dancing and chanting. Before long the sounds coming out of my throat and mouth sounded so powerful that I was amazed and awed. I mentioned this to the group the next time we met and was told it *was* powerful. That is the first time I ever felt that kind of power.

The conference was a valuable step for me. I can't say that I felt much JOY during the days there, except when I was practicing the healing energy. That was a sacred and JOYFUL experience for me and I did face a lot of feelings that I wasn't strongly aware of before then.

After I returned home I was anxious to try my new skills on someone who was ill. Everyone at the conference had been healthy so we couldn't really tell if what we were doing was effective. Before I had gone to Hawaii I had visited my sister in Oregon for a few weeks and had been away for a whole month. I left a plant with a friend of mine as I knew it wouldn't survive that long without care. When I returned and brought it home, I discovered it had developed some sort of rot. Parts of some of the leaves were like the worst stage of rotted lettuce. I decided to try giving it healing energy on the affected spots for just a few minutes twice a day. In two days time the spots were completely dried up yet the tiny veins that ran through the leaves were still intact.!!!! I was amazed and convinced. That plant, which is a type of lily, continues to live in my daughter's yard today. That was twenty-three years ago!!! I have found that when any living thing is healed by Love/God energy it stays healed. I believe my plant is direct evidence of that!!

All of these past experiences helped me move forward, but I still wondered what I needed to know to find JOY of a more lasting nature. I knew the vibrations of JOY are among the very highest of all vibrations so I continued to do whatever I could to raise my consciousness. I couldn't think of any major issues that I had left to work on, yet I figured there must be something standing in my way.

God has always been a major part of my life but my concept of God had changed. I felt spirit within and experienced a connection to people in a profound and encompassing way. I felt that while I didn't talk much about my beliefs, I was for the first time able to walk what I talked and I was able to live the unconditional love I had struggled for so long. I still was searching for everlasting JOY, yet living love is also a great place to be. The sum of all my experiences had brought me thus far.

After I returned from Hawaii I was seeking somebody who channeled high energies, a new experience I wanted to have. You may have heard the old saying that when the student is ready the teacher appears. I found what I was looking for right on my doorstep, so to speak. I was living on Bradenton Beach in Florida at the time. The Assistant Manager of the condos I lived in kept asking me about my trip to Hawaii. I didn't want to tell her because I figured she'd think I was crazy. She kept asking me, and one day I decided to tell her and let her think whatever she wanted to think. I told her and she didn't think I was crazy after all. She was fascinated, and she knew of a woman who channeled and also gave weekly classes.

I started attending the classes and it was an impressive experience for me. The spirits Marlene channeled led the group in guided imagery, using a lot of color and geometrically shaped figures. The images also sometimes related to the chakras. One night I had invited a young woman who was a massage therapist to go with me to the class. As we drove there we were talking about my profession and she asked me, "What causes mental illness?" I told her no one really knew for sure but there were different theories about what the causes might be. During the channeling one of the spirits that was coming through said, "Some of you are wondering what causes mental illness," then she went on to say that it was basically a fragmentation of the personality. That was a surprise!! I went to Marlene's classes the entire time I lived in the

Bradenton area (about two years). I had not worked on a full time basis but had done some private practice and some consultation, and I figured from my bank account it was time I went back to full time work. I looked all over the Bradenton/Sarasota area because I loved being on the beach so much. I couldn't find anything in the whole area that seemed to "fit" me and pay well enough. There were some openings at the Sarasota Hospital, but every one I applied for got taken by someone else with the exact qualifications. I was beginning to feel desperate as my daughter had come home and was unable to work. One night in the channeling class I asked one of the spirits about the jobs at the hospital I wasn't getting, and what I was told was, "Well if you want what's not right for you, you might be able to get one, but there's a lot of strife in that organization right now."

I had been unable to find a meaningful job in the beach areas and I went to visit my former retirement home clients in Orlando. It was just after Christmas and I had small gifts for them. While I was there I stopped by to see a social worker peer. She told me another social worker, Brenda, from the local hospice had been looking for me the day before. She had found the resume I had sent when I was looking for a part time job after I had closed the retirement home a few years before I moved to the beach. The hospice needed a counselor, and my friend Liz had told her I was in Bradenton and wouldn't be interested. We called Brenda within the next few minutes and, as things will happen when they are right, everything fell into place.

I was hired as a hospice counselor, and within a week I was invited to move into a coordinator position which paid much better. This was my first opportunity to work with the terminally ill. I had had a few deaths in my Retirement facility, but most people stayed healthy because of the holistic program.

I fit right into my now work in a seamless manner as I had used the hospice philosophy of treating the whole person at the Retirement Home. I learned a lot from my patients and from the staff. Death no longer held any fear for me. I couldn't have done that type of work when I was young; I just wasn't ready for it. Eventually I was asked to create a comprehensive bereavement program for the organization, and I believe it was one of the most creative and complete programs in the country at the time. We were then the fourth largest hospice in the entire United States in the early 90's. It was an exciting opportunity for me and I stayed with the organization until administrative changes caused most of my peers to leave. I didn't want to stay anymore after that.

I missed the channeling sessions I had gone to in Sarasota and was looking around for someone else who channeled on a high spiritual level. One night I had gone to a small informal art group that I belonged to. We had a speaker for the evening who was a psychic and gave a demonstration of psychometry. We each gave him a personal item to hold, and from the vibrations he gave each of us a reading. He told me several things that were right on target and his eyes looked multi-faceted to me. I had the impression he was a very spiritual man. I found out from another artist that he gave classes three times a week in his home, which was just a few miles from mine. I decided to join in.

This started a segment of my journey that was to last for many years. Gordon Banta (whom I mentioned earlier), was everything I had been looking for in a spiritual teacher. He walked what he talked. He was kind to everyone he met, and was the least mercenary of any person I knew. He channeled the Archangel Michael when I first started the classes, and sometimes he would channel for hours. He had to stop channeling the Archangel Michael as the vibratory level was so high it was damaging to his body. After that he channeled mostly Native Americans such as Quanah Parker and Lone Wolf. At the end of each session each participant could ask two questions of her/his choice and the answer would be given them. For me it was a period of intense growth.

All of my life I have been fascinated by Native Americans and their stories. My favorite book as a child was about Indians and was called "Many Moons Ago". I was told through Gordon that I had been Native American in at least two other lives and I had at least one Indian spirit guide by the name of Red Hawk. I had painted Native American portraits for many years. The Indian spirits who came through Gordon told me that if I would paint a group of the chiefs I would be given a great gift. I did paint several of the chiefs including Quanah Parker, Red Cloud, Sitting Bull, Chief Joseph, and Osceola. I also painted less well known dignitaries on commission. The gift I was given shows in the eyes of my paintings. I have been told on numerous occasions that there is "soul" in the eyes and that the eyes are "alive," Sometimes I can feel a presence and see and feel love coming through the paper. It sounds strange but it has happened and often with people who have never met me or seen my work before. One day my daughter came into my studio where I had just started a drawing of an Indian woman. I didn't have half of the features on the paper yet. "Mom, I can feel her personality," my daughter said in amazement. This happens often with persons who are not at all metaphysical.

Other experiences that came about as a result of Gordon's classes and channeling were equally amazing and awesome. At times Gordon was surprised by the things spirits told me through him. For instance Lone Wolf, a Kiowa Chief told me that I am a shaman, like he is. Later I had the opportunity to study the Cherokee Shamanic lessons and philosophy. I was unable to go to Oklahoma to participate in the experiential training, which I have always regretted. Perhaps I will be able to still complete it one day.

Gordon Banta was an unassuming and very unconditionally loving man who was a major influence in my achieving everlasting JOY. He had lived with, and been friends with Black Elk and his tribe in Colorado. His knowledge and lore of Native Americans was extensive and he told us many interesting stories and channeled prominent Native Americans for hundreds of hours. He published two books which have many tales of their cultures. One is titled "Rainbow of Light and Color" and the other is "Eye of Light and Magic." They are published by The Mandala Press if you would care to read them.

One of the experiences I had while attending Gordon's classes occurred in relationship to another participant, Susan. Susan was a young woman who told the class that prior to meeting us she had been diagnosed with a particularly virulent form of cancer. Her parents had given her a plane ticket to go to John's Hopkins Medical Center to see if there was anything that could be done for her. They had sent her off by herself, so she had no one accompanying her. When she boarded the plane a steward came by and told her to drink only water during the flight. He brought her a blanket and a pillow and was very nurturing throughout the trip. When the plane landed Susan asked a stewardess if she could please speak to the steward who had been kind to her. She didn't see him and wanted to thank him. The stewardess told her, "We have no stewards on this flight." When she got to John's Hopkins and tests were run, the cancer was gone.

After Susan told us her experience, I kept getting this image in my head. It was very clear and repetitive. I knew somehow that this was her "steward". For a while I didn't tell anyone about it, but it kept appearing and I finally told the class about it. They all wanted me to draw a sketch.

I didn't want to because I was afraid it would be all wrong. Finally, however, I took the chance and with some hesitancy I showed it to Susan. When she saw it she gasped and said it looked just like him. Could this really have happened? Only if you believe in angels and only if you believe in miracles!!! So many extraordinary experiences have happened to me since then that I no longer question them. Each one has been a small step toward lasting JOY!!!

Gordon crossed over to the other side in 2008 after heart failure. I will never forget the memorial his friends gave for him. It was on a beautiful spring day on a lake in Winter Park, Florida. After the planned service, friends got up to pay tribute to Gordon, sharing their love and memories. As they did so the sky filled with perfect images of white feathers, like nothing I had ever seen before or since. There was also one round cloud and on the inside of the cloud was a flawless rainbow. Again like nothing I had ever seen before. There is absolutely no question in my mind that he was there with us, letting us know he was there and all was well.

I want to tell you about two long and fulfilling trips I took out west, driving all over the country. The first journey was with my good lifetime friend, Mary Grove. She is like me, in that we both like to take the back roads and see the countryside. I had never driven any further west than Texas and had a yearning to see more of our beautiful land. We took the northern route and visited the Grand Tetons, the Rockies, and Yellowstone Park. We stayed at Yellowstone Lodge. It was a wondrous experience especially as I chased a majestic elk through the woods of Yellowstone with my trusty camera and watched him run and then suddenly stop, turn around, and pose for me in a fantastic posture. I felt like a real wildlife photographer. Pure JOY!!! I loved it!!!

It took us weeks to get to Oregon via the Oregon Trail as we stopped along the way whenever we had the urge. We finally arrived at my sister's house in Portland. Mary stayed a few days then flew back to Florida, while I stayed with my sister and her family for a visit, then continued on my journey by myself. This was my first such venture. I camped out, sometimes sleeping in a tent and sometimes in my Crown Victoria station wagon, which was comfortable, and which I had purchased specifically for the trip. I had never even built a fire in my entire life. I was 65 years old at the time.

I drove down the Oregon coast enjoying the gorgeous scenery, taking my time, building campfires and cooking on them. I had to account to no one for perhaps the first time in my life; at least not for an extended period of time. I could travel as long as my money lasted. I had saved three thousand dollars of vacation funds from my last job and I stretched it out for three months. I think I came home with maybe twenty dollars in my pocket. I didn't live luxuriously, but then I didn't want to.

I traveled along the California coast visiting the Redwood forests, and lingering for a few days. I wrote what I call some "ramblings" which I have included at the back of the book, if you would like to read them. I wrote at a picnic table surrounded by the huge sentinel trees in lovely autumn weather. In addition to viewing the scenery I also visited numerous art galleries, Native American Museums, and other interesting attractions. I was literally having the time of my life. I had no set schedule and sometimes I would drive all day and well into the evening, only stopping when there was something I wanted to see or photograph. One day while driving along a road in California I got a quick glimpse of an elk. I turned around and went back. Framed by a stand of trees was a majestic elk surrounded by a harem of at least ten females. What a tremendous photo I got of them.

One of Gordon Banta's nephews lived in the high desert of California but worked in Los Angeles. He allowed me to stay in his lovely home for a week and explore the area. Again I took lots of pictures and saw a good part of the country that I had never had a chance to see before. I befriended his cat "Elliot" who was fed by a neighbor when Tom was away. I think he was glad to have my company, however, for the brief time I was there.

When I left California I headed to Arizona and the Grand Canyon. The colors and the magnitude are mind boggling, and it is impossible to capture on film. Nothing can take the place of actually being there. One of the things that totally amazed me throughout the whole trip was the astounding variety and size of rocks everywhere in this fair land. I also went to Window Rock (speaking of rocks) and visited the Navajo and Hopi Reservations. I was fortunate to be there at a time the Hopi were having a festival and was allowed to take pictures of their dances. Usually photos aren't allowed.

After leaving California and Arizona, I headed for Albuquerque, New Mexico. I stayed ten days with a high school teacher, Joe, and his partner, a Pueblo Indian artist, Anthony Edaakie. Anthony makes beautiful Native American pottery. I was amazed at the precision without the use of tools or guides. Everything was free hand and appeared perfect to me. I met Joe and Anthony through Joe's mother just before I left Florida to go on my trip. She had suggested that I give them a call when I was in New Mexico. I called and they invited me to come out to their home and I ended up staying with them. They took me to visit pueblos and ceremonies and the Indian Cultural Center, and I was privileged to meet a good portion of Anthony's family. It was a heart warming experience and we became good friends. I stayed with them for ten wonderful days. They visited me later in Florida and North Carolina, and I went back to see them on my second journey west.

On my slow return to Florida I was taking unknown roads that were going in the general direction and appeared to be secondary roads not likely to come to dead ends. I had been heading south when I saw a highway going east that looked promising. I took a turn left and knew I was headed toward home, but that's all I knew. After I had gone a few miles I saw a sign that said "Quanah Parker Highway". Quanah was the Indian spirit that Gordon Banta had channeled most often. You can imagine my surprise and delight!!!! A few hours down Quanah Parker Highway I saw a state park sign and decided to go and stretch my legs a bit. Again I was amazed because there on the park grounds was Quanah Parker Lake. I had no idea these places even existed. Quanah had advised me through Gordon that he and Lone Wolf would be riding with me to keep me safe and keep my wheels turning. I drove 11,000 miles altogether and had only one minor car problem which was taken care of in fast order. It was a phenomenal, incredible trip and I arrived home a changed woman. I'm not sure exactly how I was different but I know something magical had happened to me during those three months. Somehow I felt a soft quiet inside and definitely a step closer to everlasting JOY!!

Two summers later I took another trip west. I didn't go as far west that time but went to Santa Fe, New Mexico, for a Mental Health conference, and a visit to my friends in Albuquerque. I drove the southern route and stopped on the way at Palo Duro Canyon in the Texas panhandle. The Comanche Indians had hidden out in the canyon for years eluding the US Army. Quanah Parker was their chief. They were the last tribe to be forced onto a reservation in Oklahoma. When the Army finally found them they shot all of the tribe's one thousand horses, their only wealth. They surrendered at that point and Quanah later became an advocate for the tribe in Washington, D.C.

Quanah's mother Cynthia Parker was a white woman who was captured by the Kiowa's from her home in Texas when she was a small child. Cynthia was given to Chief Nokomis of the Comanche tribe and she became his bride. Quanah was her oldest child and she had another son and then a daughter several years later. Both Cynthia and the little girl were recaptured by the Army in a raid, and taken back to her people in Texas. Cynthia did not want to be there. She yearned for her adopted people, the Comanche. The child soon died of a white man's disease and Cynthia refused to eat and died of starvation.

An amphitheater at Palo Duro Canyon was used to portray the settlement of Texas, and one of the roles in the play was Quanah Parker. I hadn't known about the production but I decided to go, and it was well done. I had planned to camp out in the canyon that night, yet I hadn't set my tent up before the presentation of the play. It was a good thing that I didn't because just before the end of the performance it started to thunder and lightening, and the rain came down in torrents. I was forced to sleep in my car. The storm went on and on with the most fantastic display of heavenly fireworks I have ever seen. I truly felt the Indian spirits were making a celestial gift just for my benefit!!!

On this trip my friends from Albuquerque took me to Acoma Pueblo, the Santa Fe market, and many other interesting places.

We visited Old Town in Albuquerque, Native American festivals, and even an outdoor opera at the Amphitheater in Santa Fe. We had a wonderful time with all the activities and family gatherings. Anthony's family adopted me into his own. I was honored to be called "grandmother."

Another of the fun things I did on that trip was to camp out in a very primitive camping site near Durango, Colorado. This was close to Mesa Verde State Park where the ancient cliff dwellings of the Anasazi Native American culture, who seemed to disappear off the face of the earth, are located. It was burning at the time I was there so I wasn't allowed to visit. The State Park where I stayed was utilized mostly at night for people passing through, so I never got to meet anyone. They generally came roaring in around midnight and were up and away by early light. Deer and elk wandered through my campsite and I looked for bear but none came my way. I spent time playing my Native American flute and for a time I would be "answered" back by a deep bass drum. I tried to locate where it was coming from, yet I could never find it. During the daytime there were two park rangers who would come and talk with me. They thought it was "so cool" that I was camping out on my own and making such an extensive trip by myself.

The two western trips truly did make a definite change in my life and I know they were part of my journey, not just to a different part of our grand and glorious country, but to a different part of myself. There is something that is "freeing" to be in a new environment where the people you meet are not the ones you associate with almost every day.

I went to work at the local hospital part-time (which sometimes turned out to be full-time) after I returned home from my last trip. I had enjoyed being in the mountains on my trips and I was thinking I might like to live in the mountains again. Most of my adult life had been spent in the flat land of Florida and I felt maybe I was ready for a change.

The following summer I went to Franklin, North Carolina, for a vacation and looked around to see where I would like to live. I loved the woods and nature and the smoking Smoky Mountains, which seem very mystical to me. I decided that I would like to be somewhere around Franklin. It took me a year before I was ready to move and then a friend of my son Chip, who lived in Franklin, found me a small temporary cottage in a little cove away from everyone. It was lovely with a deck and a barn and a pond right in front of the house. I could paint on the deck while I had views of the mountains and woods, and listened to the tadpoles, becoming frogs, practicing their newfound croaks. It seemed to me that they were surprised to hear those big sounds coming out of their small bodies. It was fun and very amusing.

What wasn't funny at first were loud noises coming from close by at night. With my hearing problem I sometimes have trouble distinguishing where sound is coming from. I knew it was close, and it was scaring me because I didn't know what it was and I was out in the woods all by myself. Every night it was the same thing. I decided fairly quickly that it wasn't anybody trying to break in, because no one did, and I'd hear the same noises each time. I finally realized it was coming from under the floor and also that it must be a family of possums or skunks that didn't like me tromping around over what they perceived as their territory. Soon after that I started stomping stridently on the floors every evening and sure enough after about a week whoever it was moved out, lock, stock, and everything. No more loud noises at night.

For two months after I moved to Franklin I would go to the grocery store and/or gas station or sometimes walk in the woods, yet I couldn't wait to get back to my sanctuary and alone time. I wasn't ready to be with people. During this period I made a decision to go back over my life mentally, taking each year and each person that I remembered from that year and analyzing my feelings for each one. I wrote down all the names and the feelings of love, caring, or anger. It took me about three weeks to complete and then I wrote a ritual for a ceremony for myself. I wanted to honor those individuals who had contributed love to my life and to forgive those who had hurt me. I also wanted to forgive myself for any intentional or unintentional hurt that I had caused anyone else. I set a date and time for the ceremony and read the ritual aloud, giving it emotional relevance. I had cut up pieces of paper with the names I had thought about and I burned the notes as I honored or forgave them and watched the wind carry away the ashes. I had released all of the "old stuff" that was still hanging around. I felt cleansed and ready to move forward with my life.

I soon found a spiritual community in Franklin. Several people were doing "hands on healing" for anyone who came every week to a room in the library. This was the nucleus of a larger group who became my friends. In addition to the healing activities we often met for drumming circles, meditation groups, workshops, potluck suppers, and any excuse to get together. There wasn't much entertainment of the usual sorts in the smaller mountain communities, so people got together more often than in larger towns and cities. It was a different lifestyle and there was more personal interaction. I liked it a lot.

A "Wellness" Farm owned by Sue Blair opened soon after I moved to North Carolina. It is located between Highlands and Franklin. Sue teaches therapeutic horseback riding for children and sometimes for older women. It has a wonderful Lodge for Workshops, gatherings of all kinds, a humongous teepee, and a barn, as well as acres of mountain wooded land and waterfalls and trails. Sue has always been generous with her place and my grandchildren and I spent many wonderful hours climbing the mountains and playing in the clear mountain stream. I met many lovely and interesting people there. I would like to mention Ed and Linda Carlson who became good friends of mine. Ed developed a program called "Core Health" as a method of utilizing Qi energy to heal physically and emotionally without having to go through the painful memories. Core Health is now available in many locations. You will find the Website in the appendix. Ed and Linda are both fantastic and loving people and there are some well-known individuals who have gone through the program and have found it tremendously helpful.

Another individual who came to Carpe Diem Farms is Richard Schulman. Richard is a metaphysical composer who creates beautiful intuitive music and soul portraits based on an individual's vibrations. He attended many functions in the Asheville area and I heard him on several different occasions. I am including his website which you will find in the appendix. He is the person who introduced me to the Inca Medicine Wheel. I will be forever grateful to him.!!!!

Smoky Mountain Mental Health Center needed a part-time therapist and I went to work for them twenty-six hours a week. It was a terrific place to work, and I was very happy there. One of the new experiences I had there was being the female counselor for a male domestic violators group. I had done a multitude of women's groups and some were for abused women, yet I hadn't done any groups for men abusers. These were guys who were ordered by the Court to come to the group, every week for three hours a week, for six months. This amount of time and the threat of jail if they didn't attend regularly gave us some "teeth." At first we used an educational model, mandated by the State of North Carolina, but as they loosened the reins a bit we began to make it much more therapeutic in nature. The men were mostly early offenders and their chances were better, at that stage, for some real change. The attitudes toward women were interesting to me, and most of them shifted their attitudes considerably during the six month period. Most of the men were able to grow as they observed how a healthy woman responded to them, and as they saw a healthy interaction between the male therapist and me. Many of these men had been abused as children and visualized themselves as victims. Some of the wives and significant others were also abusive; some seriously so. We had only two recidivists during the two years we did the class. I don't know whether the participants were able to stay out of trouble after I came back to Florida or not. I like to believe the learning was permanent.

Another glorious experience that occurred during my stay in North Carolina was an invitation to join a Women's Spiritual Group. Linda Carlson was my sponsor and we had women from all over the United States and other countries around the world. Each week we would get together on a conference call with a subject to discuss that we had all agreed upon earlier. There were eight members in the group and everyone got a chance to participate. About every six months the group would split and there would be some of the people we already knew and there would also be some new ones as well. We had very accomplished and successful women as members, and everyone was interested in becoming evolved personally and spiritually. In addition to the conference calls we e-mailed each other almost every night. I was amazed how much seemed to come through the e-mails and conference calls on an emotional level, and how intimately we got to know each other. It was the first time in my lifetime I had belonged to a gathering of women who were so totally supporting of one another. There was *no* competition among the members, no rivalry, and there was a much unconditional love expressed. We did finally meet each other face to face. Eighteen of us met in Sedona, Arizona for a long and fantastic weekend. The group consumed quite a bit of wine and did a lot of talking and laughing. There was a lot of humor and hilarity and much, much JOY!!! It was a weekend of JOYOUS highs!!!!! I was nearly "there". I felt it and I knew it!!!!

My family was mostly still in Florida except for my oldest son who is a pilot and had moved to Dallas, Texas, to be close to his company. Every few months I would drive to Florida to visit my daughter and son and grandkids. After one visit I was driving back to Franklin, it was getting late and I found myself becoming sleepy. I have discovered that if I keep my mouth in motion I can always stay awake. Since I can only eat so much, I usually opt for singing and I use my whole repertoire of songs. This particular evening I was singing my way through everything that popped into my head, and an anthem came up that I had learned as a teenager. It goes:

First Verse

My God and I go in the Fields Together, We walk and talk as good friends should and do, we clasp our hands, our voices ring with laughter. My God and I go in the meadow's hue.

Second Verse

He tells me of the years that went before me, when heavenly plans were made for me to be, when all was but a dream of dim Perception, My God and I go on eternally.

I started singing the second verse when all of a sudden I was seeing God in the creative process, loving the new creation She/He was bringing into form. Vibrations full of sound and color, putting a bit more of this and a bit more of that until all the sound and hue are just right for the being just brought into life. This form is me. I realize while this creation is in process that God has made all of us in this manner with thought, intent and unconditional love. All the hopes and dreams that each of us have as we lovingly create something new and exciting. I realized that God is my real and true parent, and throughout the entire experience tears of joy were running down my face as I continued driving along. I had finally "got it" on some very profound level. I had finally reached the very core of my being!!!! This was truly an epiphany for me and the emotional and spiritual awareness of my ascension into everlasting JOY!!!! I was finally "HOME".

Once we know that we are made with unconditional love and JOY on our unconscious as well as our conscious levels, we reach that internal core of full JOY, the vibration that we are love and loved in the finest definition of the word. Always it is there no matter what other feelings are experienced. We can feel it humming away under everything else. We can always tap into it and there is NO DOUBT!!!! If we aren't aware of its existence within us, then we know there is still some conditioning we have not yet become aware of, and that means there is still work to do.

PART TWO

Problematic Issues and Emotions

I am going to talk about the feelings and issues and problems that most often get in the way of our human emotional and spiritual growth. All of us come into this life knowing our connection to a higher dimension where love abides, but we have been conditioned from soon after birth (if not in the womb). We absorb the emotions and attitudes that surround us each day, and we fail to realize that these are "learned" and are not our real self's feelings as well as beliefs and attitudes. Some of our emotional patterns even appear to be inherited through generations of family patterning in our genes. That means that a lot of old "stuff" is in our very cells and our unconscious. Each cell has its own consciousness and intelligence. We can indeed access this information, and we can become whole and who we really are.

We all have our own set of problematic issues. Our perceptions, environment, genetic makeup, and experiences are different, and what may be traumatic for one person may not affect another to the same extent or at all. The issues below are common, though I may not have mentioned or focused on something that is a major issue for you. The solutions however are the same and can be applied to your difficulty.

Fear

There is one basic fear that we are all born with and that is the fear of falling. Even tiny babies have this fear. All other fear is learned. I believe that everything that is negative is fear-based, and everything that is unconditional love is without fear. Anything that is learned can be unlearned. Our greatest fear of all is death. Death is about the fear of change and the unknown. It is also about being alone, because for a child it is synonymous with dying, and we often bring that fear along with us into adulthood. In addition, we are often afraid of changing because we don't know who we will be if we aren't who we think we are now. Sometimes we are fearful that there will be "nothing" left if we give up the layers of conditioning that are wrapped around the real core of our true being.

Often when we give up or release an old pattern, there is a period that is known as existential anxiety, and we may feel an emptiness. However, it doesn't last long and what will come afterwards in place of the old feeling or emotion will always be better. Once we realize that this is a natural part of the change process, it becomes easier to live through it. I still experience a short time of this anxiety when I make an inner change. As I recall, it has never lasted more than a day or two at the very most.

I would like to mention here that in analogy our conscious mind is about the size of a grapefruit and our unconscious mind is the size of an ocean. We can never run out of material to work on even though it does become pain-free after we reach a certain point. There are always new information and issues to deal with and new life stages that require us to make shifts in our consciousness. If we become static then we are not fully alive!!! There are new issues every day. This is what makes life a menu of variety and keeps it exciting.

I have been told that I am forever young in my mind and I believe this is true for anyone who becomes their true JOYFUL self. To me there is nothing more beautiful in the entire world than to watch the human spirit struggling to be free. Free of fear and free to be. In Part IV I will tell you step by step how to achieve freedom.

Judgment

Judgment can be negative or it can be positive, right? Thin is good, fat is bad, love is good, hate is bad, and so on and so on. We learn judgment almost from our very first breath. We learn it from gestures, expressions, body postures, as well as from verbalizations. It becomes deeply ingrained in our conscious and our subconscious minds. I have come to the conclusion that most, if not all, of negativity is based on judgmental thinking. I cannot think of an instance where negative thought has not come from some obvious or subtle judgment. Most humans tend to judge themselves, as well as others, too harshly. We think we are too short, too tall, too fat, to thin, too careless, too rigid, too shy, too aggressive, too wimpy, etc., etc. Most of us are aware of our harsh judgments but I am convinced that most everyone acts upon very subtle evaluations that influence our daily lives to a far greater degree than we usually realize. When I first began to be aware of ways in which I beat myself up, I would find myself feeling rotten at times, for no apparent reason. Once I started tracing my thoughts to what I had been thinking just a few minutes before, I would notice the negative feeling and I would always find some subtle negative thought behind it. Once in a while it might be a positive judgment which has negative as the opposite side of the coin and is therefore the same!!!!! We need to delete good and bad and just have "it is what it is".

We cannot find everlasting JOY within us and carry around judgment. It just doesn't work. This is a MAJOR, MAJOR issue. Everything works together, yet if I had to name one thing, I believe I would say Judgment is the biggest stumbling block to finding lasting JOY. Think about it seriously. Do a self inventory. We have the power to change our "old stuff" selves. We do not have the power to change our core of being and I know of no one who would want to.

Great suffering comes from judging ourselves. In my family I was taught that girls were not to be aggressive or to express anger. Anger was considered to be "not nice" so I pushed most of it down to my subconscious or I "swallowed it". Does this sound familiar to you? Anger was not only frowned upon but also punished by guilt, and after my mother quit the guilt trips then I took over the job and did it to myself, just like so many of the folks I know did, or do still.

When my marriage started to fall apart my buried hostilities started coming to the surface and I began to feel terrible anxiety. I wanted to run away from myself, and of course, I couldn't. I really didn't know what was causing the anxiety and with it went horrendous insecurity. It was the worst time in my adult life because I had no idea who I was and it was truly "hell". It took what seemed like a long time for me to even recognize my anger and longer for me to own it and know it was okay to feel it. I was my own judge, jury, and executioner. It takes some heavy work for most of us to replace our judgmental thinking to nonjudgmental thoughts. I have to admit I was skeptical about the ability to make these changes, but my determination won out.

I do believe retraining is not enough. The first piece has to be the willingness to shift our self concept so that our self-esteem is higher. You will understand how to do this as we go around the Inca Medicine Wheel in Part IV. At the same time we are improving our self image we can also do the reframing. The way I did it was to first become aware of the judgmental thought about myself or anyone else. Then I would use the word WHOA!! That would stop me in my tracks and disrupt the unwanted thought. The next step would be to change my thinking to something happy or something I was excited about. At first the old unwanted thought would often come slipping back in, but the more I caught it, the quicker I would say WHOA!!

It does take time to decrease and delete our negative thinking but you will see that learning to control our thoughts is on the highest level of the multidimensional Inca Medicine Wheel. The Inca civilization perceived that learning to control our thinking processes is a spiritual issue and of a high spiritual order. To perceive without judgment is to stop labeling things as good and bad. It is difficult and requires patience, so don't be discouraged. Remember you are disrupting a lifetime of thought and emotion and it just doesn't go away overnight: you will find that it is so worthwhile. Inner peace and comfort are your rewards before you find everlasting JOY!!!!

I would like to point out that while I am writing about different emotions, issues and attitudes separately, they are not discrete. We often have mixed feelings, and judgment can carry different emotions with it. It has been said by some in the psychological field that there are only two real emotions—love and fear. I am inclined to agree. Think about it and I think you will see that all negative emotions are fear-based. Isn't it true that we are afraid of being hurt, of being wrong, of being nothing, of losing what we have or don't have. Then there is the fear of death, of the unknown, of unworthiness, of punishment. There are so many. Unconditional love, on the other hand, covers a lot of happy and peaceful feelings.

When I was young I was afraid of violent death. I can remember as a little kid of being afraid of being buried alive, which horrified me. I don't know where that even came from but it was one of my big fears. I can also remember when I was about four years old waking up at night and thinking I saw a red fox in the corner of my room. I wasn't terribly afraid of a fox but I was afraid it wouldn't go away and I hid my head under the covers.

As adults we bring at least some of our childhood fears with us and need to deal with them in the present. We feel affection as children, yet are unable to love unconditionally until we are able to love the emotions, thoughts, and attitudes that we have learned and that sabotage our feelings of worthiness on a deep level. As youngsters we are dependent for love, and when we don't receive the unconditional quality of love we think our caregivers are able to give us, we believe the fault is in us. Children often remember thinking, "Something must be wrong with me". Many of my former clients have told me they have thought this as children. We have to be able to love in an independent way to be an unconditionally loving person. That means that we know we are worthy and lovable even if no one else in the whole world loves us.

Somewhere along my pathway I lost my fear. I'm not sure when it happened, but it did. About fifteen years ago I was coming home from work and walking through my yard when I saw a snake sunning itself on a stepping stone close to my foot. Generally I would have reacted fearfully, but this time I said, very spontaneously, "Where did you come from,"? and walked on by. I surprised myself by not having any internal or external reaction either.

Later in my career two of my jobs have been with hospices, working with the terminally ill and their families. I have been with patients when they died peacefully and calmly. Most of them had strong religious or spiritual beliefs. They felt sure that there is a loving God and that there is life after death. There have been a few who were atheists or were in severe judgment about something they had done during their lifetime and death was a struggle for these people. As part of the hospice team it was my job to help the patient and his or her family resolve issues that caused the fear and anxiety related to dying.

One patient I had many years ago had terrible anxiety. She was so fearful that she gave her ex-husband a rough time because she was so demanding of his time. She did not want him out of her sight and it was driving him crazy. He had come back to their home as she had no one else to care for her. She was a very private person and it was difficult to get her to talk about what was bothering her, until one day when she asked me about God and what I believed was His nature. She wanted to know if I thought God could even forgive something like murder. Something in me went BINGO—I guessed that perhaps she had had an abortion when she was young. My thinking turned out to be right and I reassured her that I believe that God is a forgiving and unconditionally loving being. Our chaplain also made a visit of reassurance to her. She was better after that and died peacefully, a few months later. I am sure that she had resolved the issue within herself and that allowed her serenity at the end.

Judgment is, I believe, the strongest negative factor that keeps us from experiencing everlasting JOY. Again I would like to stress that we make such subtle evaluations of ourselves that it takes a lot of work and increasingly sharp awareness to catch the harshness with which we sabotage ourselves. It is like we have a small judge on our shoulder telling us what we should and shouldn't do, and what we should and shouldn't think and feel. Sometimes we believe that if we chase the "judge" away we won't have anyone to "keep us in line".

Freedom from restriction can be scary, especially if we've had rigid limits growing up. It has been my experience, however, that when the do's and don'ts are removed (and it is always a gradual process) then individuals become much more loving and are less apt to do anything hurtful or harmful to someone else, or to themselves. What we are basically doing is removing the outside "clutter" of our learned conditioning which came from our early caregivers (usually our parents) and reaching into the very central part of our being, which is always love and JOY!! When we are able to reach that part of ourselves, that is what we find. It is a shining, glorious, fantastic epiphany!!! It is coming HOME in the truest sense of the word, and who among us doesn't long for that. It is warmth and JOYFULNESS!!!!!

One of our major fears is that if we delete our personal history (our learned conditioning) then there will be nothing left. We will be an empty space, a vacuum of no thing. This could not be further from the truth. The core of our self is always love and JOY. It is not so much that we need to be loved, but that we need to love. Once we are able to see and feel love for ourselves, then we are able to love all others, as we are all one.

When our eyes are opened we see not only the beauty within but also the beauty without. It cannot be otherwise. We become vulnerable when we open to love and JOY. Whenever we are closed, hurt cannot penetrate, but neither can the good things come in. Allowing love and JOY to touch the heart of us means we become vulnerable. Our vulnerability is no longer the risk it once was, however, because loving our self means we are not devastated by our losses. Loss is always difficult and there will be losses in everyone's life yet the sense of it is more like an empty space that may ache, but does not leave us shattered.

Trust

Most if not all of us have wounds from childhood when we trusted someone we loved to be unconditionally loving toward us, and they unintentionally walked on our tender feelings with insensitive footsteps. These people we love as little ones rarely mean to hurt, yet they do, and because our love is a dependent love we are left wounded and bleeding. Some of us, somewhere inside our selves, made a decision that we wouldn't allow the hurt to happen again. We started building walls and defenses to keep others away and we managed very well to do that. We kept out the hurtful emotions, but we also kept out the good, warm, and comforting feelings. We feel very alone when we erect this kind of defense, yet we usually tell ourselves we don't care. Many of us spend our lives defending our castle walls. We have archers at every opening in the strong battlements and anyone who comes too close we let the arrows fly, or we go deep within the castle walls so no one will see us and think that nobody is home.

Most of us don't go to that extreme, but my experience has shown me that there is a continuum with fear of abandonment at one end and fear of domination at the other end. We all fall somewhere along that line with no fear of either abandonment or domination in the middle of the continuum. This is a place of perfect trust, a place that most of us have to work at to reach because, of course, we are who we need to trust the most. How can we learn to trust our self if we were not able to trust those we depend on. So you see everything comes back to us. We cannot "fix" anyone else, or, for that matter, we cannot *change* anyone else. Everything negative that happens to us as children increases the likeliness of negative reactions in our selves.

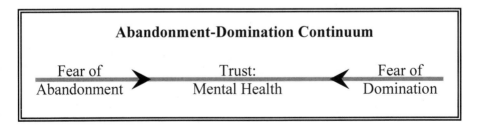

55

Along our conscious journey to be whole and loving we need to open the gates, turn the archers into a welcoming committee, and come out of hiding. I have had a visual image of myself pulling open my solar plexus area and saying, "Okay God, here I am, all of me, nothing hidden". Dangerous business it seems, yet it allows love, JOY, and peace to come in. We can't open up all at once, but we can open up a little at a time as we begin to delete judgment and embrace what we have viewed as unlovable in ourselves. It is all a process, an inner journey into the core of beingness. When we don't trust ourselves, we don't trust others. When we don't trust others, we don't trust ourselves. It is the proverbial vicious circle, and it is a good place to begin.

We can ask ourselves if we trust our love for someone dear to us, to be always kind, to be unconditional, to be consistent. How often can we truthfully answer "yes"? Remember if we say "no", there must be no judgment attached. It is all growth and it is all right to be wherever we are in our process.

To learn to trust we must realize that the feelings, thoughts, and actions that we dislike (and even hate) have served us well, and have in some way helped us survive and get to where we are today. We truly need to embrace these feelings and give appreciation for them. This is where healing and forgiveness come from. I would suggest you look at the things you have been beating yourself up about and analyze what they have accomplished for you to get where you are right this moment. Pat yourself on the back for figuring out how to help yourself survive, and appreciate your will to make your life workable!!!!! It is quite amazing how we manage, even as little kids, to come up with behaviors that help us to get along in the world. Start right now to give yourself gratitude and wonder every day that you are so clever and bright that you have made it thus far and have done quite well.

Self Worth

The bottom line is always insecurity, a lack of self-worth. Insecurity is based on the known (conscious) and the unknown (unconscious) emotional substance of what we don't like in ourselves. It doesn't matter if we don't know what we don't like, because we feel insecure even when we don't know what is hidden that we are rejecting. It just means that something is so repulsive to our self concept that we can't allow our self to even be aware of it. So we put up blocks to keep from knowing what it is. I especially remember one hospice family who had a father who was dying of cancer. His daughter was caring for him in his last days. The morphine he was taking for pain was giving him hallucinations, and he was quite a hand full. The daughter was divorced and had no one to help her. There was a brother who lived in the area and the caregiver explained to me that her brother was very arrogant and would have nothing to do with helping out. I asked about the family's early relationships and I saw that there were some problems there. We discussed the attitude of arrogance that seemed to be an overriding feature of any family interactions including the brother. I suggested that arrogance is often a defense when a person is actually feeling insecure, for when we feel good about our selves we have no need to be either arrogant or submissive.

I encouraged the caregiver sister to invite her brother over and explore their problems in a loving, caring way. They did get together and it turned out better than expected. It came out that the brother had always felt left out of the family. He felt like he was standing on the outside looking in, and it hurt badly. He pretended it didn't matter and the family had always assumed he didn't care. When all this came out the caregiver asked for forgiveness and put her arms around the brother and hugged him and invited him back into the family. They became reunited and the brother became a willing co-caretaker for the dad who was so pleased that his strong and caring son was with him during his final days.

As we learn to embrace the entirety of our range of emotions, thoughts and actions we integrate them into our being so that they no longer have control over us and we choose how we want to respond rather than reacting to our perception. The more we encompass the totality of our conditioned emotions and reactions the more secure we become within our selves.

Guilt

Guilt is the way we punish ourselves for something we have been taught we should or shouldn't feel, think or do. It is a learned reaction and as I mentioned above we often do it to ourselves long after someone else triggers the guilt reaction. Sometimes we punish ourselves with guilt for years after an infraction.

My earliest memory of guilt was at the ripe old age of four. During the early summers at the Inn in Pine Grove Furnace in Pennsylvania my parents bought groceries and supplies for the Inn at the general store which was in a large log cabin. I was often with them when they shopped, and they always told the proprietor to "charge" the supplies at the end of the transaction. I happened to love licorice sticks and usually they would add a piece or two to the grocery order.

One day, all on my own, I decided I wanted some licorice. I took myself, without permission, down to the store (which was maybe a quarter of a mile away) and marched up to the counter and told the proprietor I wanted two pieces of licorice. Without questioning me he got the candy and asked me how I would like to pay for it. I said, very firmly "just charge it". He put it in a bag and I walked back home. I expected to be caught and punished, not only for buying the candy and charging it, but also for going by myself that distance from home. Maybe my very first act of complete independence!!!!

No one EVER said anything to me about it. I never knew if my absence went undetected and all the several people who looked out for me thought one of the others was watching me. I never knew if the store owner even charged the licorice to my parent's bill or if my parents noticed an extra charge on their bill for two pennies. At any rate I suffered guilt for years because I went free when I had done something I knew my parents would have disapproved of. You see how early I learned to be my own judge jury and executioner!!!! The long-term guilt, of course, was my punishment. It doesn't have to be anything big, but something unbelievably simple can affect us for a long, long time.

One of the ways we can stop chastising ourselves is to do the same thing we did with negativity. It starts with awareness. Once we become cognizant that we are feeling guilty, we can use the WHOA word again and tell ourselves, "I'm not going there", or "I'm not going to do this to myself anymore" and change our thought to something positive. When we do this repeatedly we erase it from our conscious mind. It takes a while but it does work.

Grief

Everyone has grief in their lives at some time or another. We don't necessarily have to have a major loss to have grief. Sometimes we ignore our minor griefs and then we lose someone or something really important and we are devastated beyond imagination. All of the built up grief is added to our already large grief. We often do not grieve over situations like moving to a new location and leaving behind friends, family, jobs, or our home for maybe a number of years. Even though we may be looking forward to a new life it doesn't mean we don't mourn what was lost. Other events may be changing jobs, losing some physical ability, life stage changes and of course, divorce and death. At times we may not even recognize the symptoms, or we may put off our grieving because we're too busy.

I remember when I was ten years old I decided that I was too old for dolls anymore. I hadn't played with them for quite a while but they were still hanging out in my bedroom. I decided that I would put them away "for good," and as I packed them away in a box or trunk I became aware that the child I had been was gone forever. I cried a long time at that transition. I didn't really understand the full meaning of it but I certainly felt the grief.

I also became consciously aware later on that whenever I moved and started a new job I would have thoughts of being killed in an accident while driving. I would think to myself, "I've been driving for a long time now and my number may be coming up". Thoughts of this nature would just slip in my mind in a subtle way and then I'd find myself being a little bit depressed. That seemed kind of crazy because I'd like my new job or my new situation. When I became really cognizant of what I was doing I had to laugh at myself because my symptoms were really classical of the grieving process.

Death is often equated with the unknown and depression is one of the five stages of grief as defined by Elizabeth Kubler Ross[3]. Since I became aware of what I was experiencing I have consciously noted the different stages, but being aware of what will happen before this type of event has lessened the severity of the symptoms, and they usually pass quickly. The stages are as follows.

The first stage is denial, where we experience shock and are unable to believe what has happened. We are numb and anesthetized against the pain of knowing. This is our system's way of protecting us from the full painful effects which gives us time to adjust to the loss. Denial may reappear for a long time throughout the grieving process.

The next step is anger. Not everyone goes through this stage, yet if they do it can be aimed at anyone or anything, including God. Anger blocks movement forward. As long as the anger is being experienced we do not move through the other stages, but stay "stuck". Some persons may need some professional counseling to help them work through the angry feelings.

The third phase is bargaining and many individuals don't go through this stage. Yet many terminally ill people do. A terminally ill person may bargain for more time if there is an important birthday coming up, the birth of a new grandchild, or some one they want to see before they die and who can't be there right away. There are multiple reasons for bargaining, and the patient's part of the deal usually goes something like this: "God, if you'll just let me live until such and such occurs, then I'll go gladly". The interesting part is that often they do live just exactly that long and then immediately afterwards they are gone. That is why I believe we have much more control over our life and death than we usually think is possible. I've seen it too many times not to believe it.

The fourth stage of grief is depression and is the hardest to live through. It can last a long time and is difficult to deal with. It may be so severe that we don't want to do anything, not even get out of bed in the morning, or take care of the simplest tasks. It is critical at this stage that we allow ourselves to grieve and mourn, and it is also important that we push ourselves to get out and start to meet the world again. The more we understand the process and what is happening the better. Most persons during a major grief have what they describe as "crazy" feelings. This is normal. Another thing that is important to know is that the stages do not necessarily go from A to B and then on to C. In reality we may be in depression one day and in denial the next then on to acceptance and then back to depression. Everyone is different within the same basic framework, yet there are many variables. Men sometimes have a very hard time with grief, as so many have been taught that it is weak to express the more tender feelings. It is far more likely for a man to have cancer, a stroke, a major accident, a heart attack, or other catastrophic event within the first year after an important loss than it is for a woman. We all need to encourage men to express grief after a loss and help provide a supportive environment for them.

The fifth and last stage of the grief process is the final phase where we are able to let go of the person we have lost, with love, and acknowledge that while we will miss them it is okay for them to go. Letting go of someone we love is the hardest thing most of us ever have to do. It is, however, the great illusion. We don't really have a choice, yet acceptance within the psyche appears to be something we can manipulate to comfort ourselves. Great suffering comes when we are not able to let go of someone we love. Our closeness to the person who has left us, and the depth of our dependency on that person, are usually indicative of the severity and length of our grieving. This isn't true for a child, however as a parent may even have trouble wanting to stay alive for the first year after the loss of the son or daughter. Our religious beliefs and faith are also a major factor in the grieving process.

Grieving has to do not only with the person whom we've lost but also with what we will miss out on because that person is no longer physically available. With a spouse we may miss out on retirement plans, travel, couples activities and watching our children in the various stages of their lives, grandchildren, and all the special events that go along with them. When we lose a child, no matter their age, there are other events and happenings we also will not see. Sometimes we feel cheated and we do grieve over what we didn't have as well as the basic loss. The absence of physical touch may also be a large part of our grieving. We may even feel the presence of the person but miss terribly holding them in our arms; the tender or erotic touches. Grief is a normal part of life. It isn't easy and it can last for a long time. For most spouses it takes a minimum of two years to reach the acceptance stage. With a young child it can be even longer.

Attachment

On our journey to everlasting JOY it is important to let go with love (detach) from those individuals we are close to. Detachment is a very difficult task yet one which is critical to our growth process. Attachment is equal to becoming involved in a person's control issues, manipulations and other dramas. Anytime we become entwined in another person's "stuff" we become susceptible to being pulled away from our peaceful, harmonious status. When we need someone else (anyone) to meet our need for love and self worth, we cannot find everlasting JOY. Lasting JOY is based upon a gradual letting go of the necessity of depending on another person(s) for our inherent worth. Babies come into the world dependent on their caregivers for everything including love. The problem exists because most parents never learned to teach their children how to love themselves without condition, or even that it is possible that we don't have to look outside ourselves for that love. It isn't that parents don't want to give their children what is healthy and best for them, it is because they don't know how. This goes back generations, forever. To detach doesn't mean we stop loving a person, it simply indicates we don't get caught up in their unhealthy behaviors. It actually frees us up to be more loving. It's a part of the "unconditioning process" and most certainly a part of deleting judgment.

In learning to embrace and integrate our conscious thoughts, feelings and behaviors that have been problematic for us, we make "space" for unconscious material to come into awareness for us to work on. Sometimes we may be unable to get beyond our old conditioned feelings by ourselves. We may need to seek professional help for awhile. At times the pain may be too intense and we need a kind and compassionate person who knows how to get us through our discomfort with the least amount of pain, as quickly as our psyche can handle it. There are many resources in communities today. Just be sure to find someone you feel is compassionate if you go this route. I have always wanted to be as consciously aware of as much of my total experience as is humanly possible. Some folks do not, and that is okay too. Fortunately we have choices.

Projection

Projection is a common defense mechanism that we unconsciously utilize to protect ourselves from pain. What this means is that we believe that another person (usually someone close to us), is experiencing a certain feeling or thought when it really is our own emotion or thought that we have a problem owning up to. We believe we are not responsible for whatever it is and blame the other party. For instance, we may feel our partner is feeling ambivalent towards us when she/he is not at all. It is actually our own emotion projected onto the other individual that we have assumed to be guilty. The other person usually doesn't have a clue, unless we start an argument or accuse them of something they know nothing about.

I remember as a young woman going into a class and thinking that a particular man in the class didn't like me. That was crazy thinking because this guy didn't know me, and, in fact, hadn't even met me. I came face to face with my own projection and realized it was my own feeling of not liking myself. At least, even though I didn't know what to do about my insecurity at that time, I became more aware of myself and how I so obviously twisted things around.

We need to become cognizant, in our growth process, of how we handle projection and how often we do it. The best way to make sure we are not projecting is to ask the person in question if they are feeling whatever it is we may be thinking of blaming them for. It can be an eye-opening experience.

Once we stop projecting we have taken a big step forward toward eternal JOY and are taking full responsibility for our own emotional state as well as our thoughts and behaviors. To have continuous JOY humming away within ourselves we must move toward full responsibility for our own self, our own life.

Needing to be Right

I would just like to mention before we move on that in relationships some of us have a problem with needing to be "right". In an argument neither partner is willing to let go of their own position, so it is difficult, if not impossible, to resolve. When I was faced with this behavior by my therapist, I said, "If I give in, then what do I get out of it"? It was one of the hardest things for me to let go of. I tried it, however, and much to my amazement, found that I didn't lose a thing, and I gained a relationship. I may have lost the battle but I won the war and we were both much happier. This may not be a problem for you, but for me it was.

Masculine and Feminine

All of us have masculine and feminine aspects of ourselves, as I'm sure you know. In western cultures our society has generally negated the opposite gender of our physical reality within ourselves which we have mostly all experienced. Males have rarely been taught to honor and love the "softer" more "tender" aspects of ourselves, nor have women been given support for the action-oriented, independent parts of their beings. This has begun to change, but it has been slow in becoming fully developed. You will note that there is no gender difference as we traverse the Inca Medicine Wheel. We approach our journey as voyagers on a holistic pathway. It is my hope that the men who have been slow to recognize and embrace the natural feminine within will begin to fully acknowledge and clarify this aspect of ourselves. Interestingly, rather than being diminished and weakened by this acceptance, men become truly strong "alpha" males as they become whole. On the other hand, women who are willing to integrate the warrior self and the independent woman are also able to "surrender" and be passive when the time is appropriate.

We become power full when we are able to integrate all of the different, clarified, essential parts of our selves. This kind of power has no ego attachment and allows equality and true relationship between partners. I suggest that women spend special time on the West side of the Inca Medicine Wheel which is the direction of the masculine Warrior and that men also invest as many hours, days, or more in the feminine North. Remember there is no time limit and we need to respect our own inner processes to move as quickly or as slowly as is necessary. It is really okay if we camp out in one direction. It is even okay if we build a house there. Judgments are not allowed!!!! We can be the tortoise and not the hare. The fact that we are on the pathway is a continual reason for celebration!!!! I am sure we have a spirit audience cheering us on. The inchworm moves in tiny increments and it gets there. That is all that matters!!!!

Ego

We don't need ego. In my opinion ego is only valuable to us if we need to be the big "I AM" because we feel insecure. We are all as important as anyone else. It is hard to let go of ego, yet it sure feels good when we realize we don't need or want it anymore. Unconditional love is the key. Unconditional love for our self makes everything feel different.

Several years ago I was teaching a course at a local college: Introduction to Psychology. There is a tremendous amount of material to be covered and I was determined to include as much "feeling" content as possible. I always wanted to help students learn the emotional/spiritual aspects of a subject, and not just didactic information.

One evening I just started talking about unconditional love in response to a question. Suddenly I noticed a deep silence, and you could have heard a feather drop in a class of forty-five people. There was not one sound in that room. Everyone was so quiet and I felt like I was holding them in the palm of my hands. It was as though each person there was reaching out for that love, and it is a hunger of all people everywhere. When it touches us even briefly we can leave our chattering minds and any other distraction, and be totally "there."

PART THREE

Chakras

I would like to interject right here a bit more information about chakra systems and the Inca chakra system in particular. Many civilizations believed in the actuality of chakra energies and it is only fairly recently that some researchers claim to have found scientific evidence supporting their existence.

Societies using the chakra energy systems include the Hindu, Tibetan, Cherokee, Inca, Egyptian, and African. All of them have similarities with some differences. The chakra colors of the different civilizations are mostly consistent although the Crown chakra for the Incas was violet while most others perceive it as white. Some psychics are able to visualize the chakra colors with the naked eye and anyone can learn to feel the energy of the chakras. Also the number of chakras varies from 6 to 12, depending on the culture. In referring to the chakra systems in this reading I refer to the Inca luminous energy systems, however these are complex and you may wish to delve deeper into the subject.[1]

The Inca (who were an empire and not a single tribe) perceived each individual person as having a luminous energy field that surrounds the body and resembles in shape the magnetic field of the earth. It transfers information into and out of the being, flowing out of the top of the head and re-entering through the feet. The chakras are a part of the luminous energy system and are described as spinning wheels of light, which send threads of energy outward to connect with other persons, animals, plants and the earth. The Incas believed that the lower five chakras receive nourishment from mother earth while the higher chakras are fueled by the sun. They also believed God is omnipresent and omniscient and flows into all life in its many forms in order to experience itself. All beings are seen as inclusive of all features of God.[1]

The chakras below are the chakra system of the Inca Indians, and we will be working with all nine chakras on our journey around the Inca Medicine Wheel.

Inca Chakra System—Chakras 1-9

Chakra #1 is the Root Chakra located around the base of the spine, and the color is red. It has the lowest, most dense vibrations of all the chakras. It is our tie to Mother Earth. It relates to a craving for security and protection, for safety and survival. It is a holding place for limitless spiritual energy, or kundalini, which lies sleeping in this chakra waiting to be unblocked so energy can flow upward. It is also connected with fear, impatience, intolerance, and greed. We will be working with the issues of insecurity as well as the other emotions that are connected to this chakra and the next three on the first two levels of the Inca Medicine Wheel.

Chakra #2 is the next lowest and dense in vibration and is located in the lower abdomen. It is connected to creativity, pleasure, sex, procreation, self-esteem, control, and morality. When this second chakra is open and balanced the individual will begin to "blossom" as a person and be sensitive and filled with potential dreams. The energy causes an inability to be grounded and stable or to set boundaries for ourselves when it is blocked. It may also cause an individual to be melodramatic and over-emotional tending to get involved in dramas or to go overboard in satisfying sensual desires. Depression may occur when this chakra is unbalanced. The color is orange.

Chakra #3 is located in the solar plexus with the energy mostly felt between the navel and the sternum's base. It is a little higher on the vibratory scale and the color is yellow. It is related to power, self-esteem, and courage. All personal growth and change begins at this chakra and is a transformative energy. It takes true courage to consciously commit to the growth process because it means facing the unknown, as well as the known within ourselves. Remember the conscious mind is in analogy the size of an orange and the subconscious the size of an ocean. That can be somewhat intimidating!!!! If you, dear reader, are on your personal journey give yourself multiple embraces, for you are indeed full of courage.

Chakra #4 is the "Heart" chakra, the site of unconditional love. There is much to learn to embrace before we reach this core, which is the real self, on the upper limits of this vibration. Compassion and the capability for intimacy are a positive result of removing the barriers of this chakra. The level of vibrations has increased dramatically. Emotions that must be embraced and integrated prior to finding unconditional love include loneliness, abandonment, grief, betrayal, and resentment, as well as a lack of generosity—some very large issues to embrace. The color of the chakra is green, the color of healing.

Chakra #5 is connected to communication, creativity, and the manifestation of dreams. This chakra is about expressing our personal truth to others. It is related to stimulating our hearts and minds with creative thoughts and experiences. It is about sharing what we are, and what we are about with others. It can be exhilarating, especially if we have been shy about expressing ourselves. In high school I suffered anytime I had to make a speech, even though I was well prepared. I would always try to be last on the agenda, although that prolonged the agony. In college I was determined to take a speech class and did in fact take Oral Interpretation. The professor was known to be "tough". The room was an amphitheater and the speaker was on the "floor" with all the other students and professor sitting above and around him or her. While she was presenting her work everyone else was evaluating her on a standard form, which was quite thorough. We had to read once or twice a week, and for the first two months when it was my turn, my knees literally knocked, and my voice shook. No practice or anything else helped. Then, magically, one day I went to the mike and unbelievably, the fear was gone (just like that) and I was never afraid of public speaking again. The really exciting part for me was that I got the highest grade in the class for the drama presentation which was an excerpt from the drunk scene in "Who's Afraid of Virginia Wolfe". I was more proud of that than almost anything else I did in college because I was the only student in the class who wasn't a speech major. Take opportunities to make your truth known, quietly, or to larger groups. Let your light shine!!!! The color is blue.

Chakra #6 is located in the mid –forehead, and, when it has been opened, is the seat of intelligence, wisdom, and intuition. It is sometimes called the *psychic eye*. It is also the center of our judgment, emotional (as compared to academic) intelligence, and the pathway to the attainment of enlightenment, and therefore everlasting JOY. The further we are able to work through the issues which clog the movement of energy to higher vibrations the closer we are to our goal of everlasting JOY. Problems that prevent us from moving into this space, keeping us blocked, relate to lack of self-discipline and inner vision as well as fearing success.

We all have intuitive abilities and I imagine we have all experienced at least a minimum number of common ones, such as knowing who is on the phone before we answer. There may have been many more that we have not recognized. Once we have worked with the issues on this level we may be in for some fantastically superconscious experiences. One I particularly remember happened while I was in Gordon Banta's classes. Spirits were telling me that I was supposed to take a pony ride across the night sky with "She Who Make It Rain or Not Rain", who would lead me to the pony in my sleep. I had a hard time visualizing this happening, yet one morning I woke up and it felt like I was on horseback and I could see the front of a saddle and every hair on a pinto pony's neck, and the neck and ears of the pony. I did not remember a ride across the sky, and the Indian spirits laughed and said they knew I didn't remember, yet I had a hard time staying on and was slipping and sliding all over the place. It was a funny picture they painted. .Meditation is especially helpful in opening this chakra, and there are wonderful guided imageries to work with.

Chakra #7 is the crown chakra. It is related to selflessness, wisdom, and integrity. It is also the site of transformation and illumination. The crown chakra is our connection to infinite consciousness which transcends worldly activity and moves us to a timeless existence which is the gateway to universal energy. The ability to access the crown chakra, as blockages are opened, brings us to the place where everlasting JOY becomes our reality. We are then able to receive guidance from higher sources and are drawn toward the mystical. Spirituality then becomes an inner experience, rather than depending on formalized religion. The color of the crown chakra for the Inca is violet.

Chakra #8 is a golden color and relates to transcendence, timelessness, bliss, and JOY outside the luminous body of the human, and is considered the source of the sacred. There is no psychological connection. This chakra is considered to be the soul's connection to spirit. It is within the human aura although it is outside the energy body. When we temporarily shift to this chakra, we are in a mystical state outside of time and space.

Chakra #9, the ninth and final chakra of the Inca Energy system, is infinite, and is related to JOY/BLISS and the return to God. It lies outside the human energy system and extends throughout the entire universe, outside of space and linear time. It is connected to the eighth chakra by a luminous cord.

PART IV

THE INCA MEDICINE WHEEL

A Walking Growth Model from Shadow/Pain to Light/JOY

Hundreds or even thousands of years ago the Inca Indians of Peru created a model of human development and potential. They envisioned it as a multidimensional Medicine Wheel which takes us through stages of emotional and spiritual growth and leads ultimately to enlightenment and mysticism. It erases old life history and karma and clears the DNA patterns that keep us from experiencing everlasting JOY. Although the charts included in this book show each level as one dimensional, it is my belief that they must be, in actuality, spiral and three dimensional.

The Inca Medicine Wheel is an amazing inner guide for human expansion on both the emotional and spiritual levels. The Incas are one of the great ancient wisdom civilizations that disappeared off the face of the earth, leaving those who follow a brilliant pathway to sacred mysteries usually unknown to ordinary people. The spiritual plane of the Medicine Wheel and corresponding Inca chakra system go beyond time and space and connect us with the sacred, "oneness" with the universe and God and with permanent unending JOY!!! I am going to share it with you as I understand it, along with my interpretations, thoughts and comments.

The directions of south, west, north, and east, each have specific aspects, as do all medicine wheels. Each direction of the Inca Wheel represents issues of emotional and spiritual development and their remedies.

On the Inca Wheel we always begin with the south direction, which on the first level of the Wheel is the wounded elemental being. On the second level the south direction becomes the wounded healer and the third level transmutes into the healer. The wounds have healed. Pain is deleted.

Next, to the west, we find warrior energy. The tasks change from the first to the second level so that there is a difference in clarity. The third level becomes the level of the compassionate, spiritual warrior, (which seems somewhat a contradiction in terms). On the third west plane there is a shift away from any violent action and/or thinking. We have found the pearl in the oyster. We have found a well of compassion for ourselves and for others; a very giant step. The west direction relates to the masculine in both men and women, yet has some different chores for each, as well as some likenesses.

The north direction is feminine and is related to the emotions. On the first level of the north direction we are caught up in intense feelings, drama, and manipulation. It tends to relate to the solar plexus chakra which may keep us in a chaotic, reactionary state of pain. It is, if you remember, the place where personal growth begins. Clarification and purification of the emotions from level one to level three brings us to unconditional love towards the upper limits on that plane.

Finally we reach the east direction which is the lodging place of judgment, of the ungenerous heart that needs opening, and the place where our "stuff" is held. Embracing and understanding the emotions from levels one to three bring transformation from rejection and lack of trust to that of acceptance and peace. We are on the edge of a major shift. Our insecurity, our dependency, and our suffering are coming to an end and everlasting, forever JOY is within our reach.

REACTIONARY HUMAN BEING

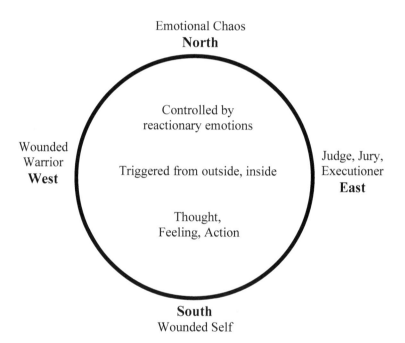

Emotional Chaos
North

Controlled by
reactionary emotions

Wounded
Warrior
West

Triggered from outside, inside

Judge, Jury,
Executioner
East

Thought,
Feeling, Action

South
Wounded Self

LEVEL I

LEVEL I: Reactionary Human Being

The first level of the Medicine Wheel is similar to the early stages of human development and conditioning. Feelings are basic and intense. They occur without prior thought and are always a reaction to a stimulus in the internal or external environment. An infant cries when she is hungry, a toddler has a temper tantrum when he doesn't get his way. Unfortunately some of these feelings and behaviors may be carried into adulthood. Sometimes we don't act them out, yet the emotions are there. Feelings that are extremely strong almost always have their roots in early childhood. If we are experiencing elemental emotions we are at their mercy and are probably uncomfortable when they arise. I expect that if you have chosen to read this book you have become much more aware of your self and may only experience this type of emotion occasionally and don't like it when you do.

The basic goal on this first level is to begin to observe the conscious emotions and thoughts, and to raise our awareness of what is taking place within ourselves. We will also begin to experience our feelings and to perhaps get glimpses of uncomfortable and painful forces that have previously been unconscious. There is little awareness of self and our behaviors appear to happen without any conscious effort or thought process. It becomes paramount during the early exploration of ourselves, to observe and note what has been felt but not perceived, and to examine carefully what is felt as it arises. Most importantly, it is the time to start embracing what we have rejected in ourselves in the past and to appreciate what it has achieved for us. Without this piece we won't move forward. The process is to first become aware of a feeling, thought, or attitude that we don't like and to allow ourselves to experience it, without judgment. The next step is to figure out how we have used this thought, feeling or attitude to protect ourselves, or to help us survive. Every time we have this particular emotion, we need to remind ourselves of how this particular experience has served us to our benefit. The last step is to embrace ourselves and give thanks to our processes for having helped us survive.

What we often notice during this process is that little "squiggles" of feeling, like small earthworms sticking their heads up out of the ground of our unconscious and then speedily going back underneath the surface of our minds. If we will observe and examine these covert emotions we will begin to recognize that here is something we are not embracing, and we need to find out more about it so we can begin to give it credit as helping us in some as yet undetermined way. It has helped us to get where we are right now. The more we track down these little "squiggles" of feeling and work with them (using the above process), the more they will come out into the light. This is how it works.

The subconscious or unconscious doesn't allow feelings, memories, or dreams, to surface unless we are ready to deal with them. Once in a while we may catch a fleeting glimpse of something and then it will be gone and we will be left wondering what it was that just went by. When that happens it is usually because we weren't ready for it. It will come back, however, when we are ready to face whatever it is. It may also come back with increasing intensity and pain. Take it as slowly as you need to and get help professionally if you can't do it alone. It doesn't mean you are weak if you need someone to help you through. It really means you are strong enough to admit that sometimes we need a hand.

South

We are now entering the Medicine Wheel on the first level in the south direction, and the wounded self feels pain and sometimes profound emotional suffering. We look to people outside ourselves to give us the love that we need and want. There is judgment and hurt over intense feelings that are not easily controlled, and we most likely punish ourselves with guilt or self rejection. Insecurity is the basic problem of all humanity and it is this south position that we return to time and time again. It is the focal point for all our other issues. The emotions on this south level are related to the first chakra which is about jealousy, loss, envy, and the will to survive. Vibrations of the root chakra are the most dense of all the chakras and when the energy is blocked by fear and rejection we cannot go forward. Dependency and attachment are major factors.

Persons who are stuck at this stage are seeking love and approval. They may feel love for someone, yet it is a love that is dependent on the other person to care for them, and cannot be maintained if that individual does not love them back. They feel devastated if the other person rejects them or leaves them for whatever reason. Trust is usually a big issue. Quite often we reach an impasse in our developmental process at the stage we would have learned to trust. This happens when we are about two years old. Our "stuckness" occurs because our parents or other caregivers were unable to give us unconditional love because they didn't get it, and their parents before them didn't give it or receive it, and so it goes for many generations. It is only in recent times that we are learning how to become whole persons, in this culture at least.

Another problem we sometimes face is our fear of transformation because we don't know who we will be if we change ourselves. We don't know who we will be without the old feelings, thoughts, attitudes and behaviors. We may be afraid that if we change that there will be nothing within us, and that is too frightening to comprehend. It takes awareness and a brave heart to make a shift toward unconditional love and embracing all of the emotional "ogres" that are in between. There may be a period of existential anxiety where we are waiting to feel whatever is new come into our awareness. This is only a short period of time, however, and understanding that it may occur makes it easier to accept. I want to assure you that underneath all of the conditioned emotions is the core of all of our beings, which is pure and unadulterated unconditional love and forever JOY.

It is here at this time and place that we need to be observant of our dependency and our attachment to others. There are questions we can ask ourselves to determine where we are with these issues: Do we need another person to feel like we are whole? Are we able to love ourselves without the approval and caring of someone else? Do we get caught up in the dramas, control, and manipulations of other people? Do we get pulled down emotionally by another individual's problems? We need to look at these issues honestly!!! It is impossible to have eternal JOY if we are dependent and attached.

We will be working on these issues on each level of the Inca Medicine Wheel, and on this first plane we become the observer. We take our very first steps towards detachment. This doesn't mean that we don't care or we don't love when we are detached. We actually are able to love without getting caught in the traps of the other person's conditioning and that is a very good feeling. It takes time to reach the point of detachment, and work. Our final step to detachment is simultaneously our first step to true freedom. I see it as a movement of great magnitude and a major shift on each and every level as we take even baby steps toward this goal. It may be a little scary to be free when we never have been before, yet it is exhilarating!!!!

We are on the first level, south direction and we need desperately to return to the wounded, isolated, small child within and ASAP bestow on this vulnerable wee being all the warmth, connection, kindness, loyalty, love peace, JOY, and serenity she/he so longs for. We also need to create importance and meaning as well. It is critical that we give these things to ourselves because we can lose everyone human to circumstance or choice. We can finally only depend on ourselves on the earth plane although God and spirit are with us always and we are never truly alone.

Spend quality time being with and communicating to your inner wounded child, listening, listening. Come back often to this first level vulnerable self and embrace, embrace, embrace. Continue to embrace until she/he is strong, healthy, loving, and JOYFUL!!

It is of critical importance today to find our core self, our love and our JOY. We attract to ourselves what we project outward, and so it is that our safety and perhaps even our survival is dependent upon drawing to us that which is loving and peaceful.

A few months ago I went to a performance given by a lovely human being who talked about her own journey and about how frightened she was as a small child. She was afraid the wind would blow her away. Her parents laughed at her for something she did or said, and told her she was "funny". She took on herself (as we all do) what her family and other persons told her she was. When she grew up she became a comedian and a singer and went into the entertainment field. This is how she had been defined by her environment. She became well known nationally, and was tops in her particular field. She married someone prominent and had lots of material possessions and thought she was happy. After a time life events took place and her life started to fall apart. She felt tremendous pain and terrible fear because she had no idea of who she really was. Over a period of time and increasing self awareness she was able to make a shift from her head to her heart. She obviously walked the path of the Inca Medicine Wheel without calling it that. Over time she came out whole. Now she travels around helping others move in the same direction.

I want to give you a channeled message from Quanah Parker that I believe is fitting for the south direction of the Medicine Wheel, and I quote, "You are unique, you are different than anyone in the whole universe. You (we) are alike in many ways, same emotions, but different experiences, differences physically. Every leaf, every blade of grass, every person is made up of molecules which have the same chemical and electrical makeup, yet even such a tiny molecule is also different and unique. Each person has their own energy vibration different from every other thing or being in the entire universe. Yet there is a place for all things, for all beings are a web of interrelationships which depend on all others to make a complete situation. Like a complete building in which each piece fits together perfectly and without any one piece would not be complete. Each of us is different as a unique part of a whole and perhaps the entire world/universe would collapse without each special life, changing the structure as birth and death occur. Back to your uniqueness which is not enough—so what if I am unique? What I need to know is that I am worthy and beautiful. Only then may I be content It is not enough to be unique. Even a clump of dirt can be unique. What does that mean unless I am of rare beauty. Few humans see ourselves as beautiful, much less of rare beauty, yet we of a different dimension see each of you as most awesome and lovely. Most humans are unable to see themselves as they truly are".

The reason for our lost vision is that the core of our beings is buried under the conditioning of the past. As we move onward we will reach a destination where we will become aware of our own beautiful self.

We prepare to leave the south on the first level of the Medicine Wheel knowing that we will be continuing to work on the same issues, clarifying as we go ahead to each of the three levels.

West

We move ahead on our pathway going westward. We have recognized our wounded, hurting self and perhaps for the first time we see that there is something to be done to stop the suffering. We don't have to remain unsure of ourselves and who we are, yet there are tasks to be accomplished if we are to reach our destination.

The west direction is the place of the warrior. It is the masculine and relates to that part of both women and men. The tasks of this direction may differ by gender, yet they are all related to issues of violence, control, attachment, dependence and fear. We prepare ourselves to take the first tentative steps where we encounter the warrior within. We find in this space the darkest of all human emotions. We may not be ready to tackle this direction so early on, so we may move to the north or east from the south. It will not go away, as we would wish, so we will have to come back to it eventually, because it is there. We must deal with it if we are to become a whole and integrated person. I am going to talk about it in sequence even though you may digress for a time.

The world in which we live and grew up is a violent world, and has been throughout most of the history of civilization. It has been mostly patriarchal and men in general tend to act out their violent, elemental, warrior personalities more than women. Wars have been fought regularly somewhere on the planet throughout most of recorded time. In addition there are many other forms of violence—slavery, sacrifice, domestic violence, sexual violence, oppression of various kinds, as well as the collective unconscious which has stored all the rage of mankind for millennia. The media of today is full of man's inhumanity to man. We cannot watch the news or TV or read a newspaper without being bombarded with stories of violence. It is no wonder that our response to this flood of brutality has been to absorb it into our very pores.

I recall early on in my career that I was asked to lead one of several minigroup therapies at a local seminar. Two of the people in the group that was appointed to me had a family member who had been murdered two years prior to their attendance at the workshop. They told about how extremely traumatized they had been since the event. They had been to several therapists without any resolution. Unfortunately, I wasn't able to help much at that point either as I wasn't able to recognize that most persons would react with a corresponding inner rage equal to that of the murderer. I like to think that I would have been able to grasp what their inner experience was if they had been clients of mine for a while. I always hoped that they found the professional who was able to help them. The saying that violence begets violence is so often true.

Another situation that I shall never forget happened when I was on call and had gone to the local hospital emergency room to see a man with severe alcoholism. During the time I was making an assessment on the man, a woman was brought into the hospital by Law Enforcement. She had just shot and killed her husband who had been brutally abusing her for many years. The police, I was told, had been called to the home dozens of times on domestic violence calls. The woman, his wife, would never sign papers that would allow the officers to pick him up and incarcerate him. Their children, who had been witnessing the abuse their entire lives, had been begging her to press charges, or leave him, to no avail. They were all gathered around watching when she had finally had enough and they watched in horror as she blew him away.

What got my full attention was that this woman was totally "out of it". I could see her and hear her and she was absolutely incoherent. She appeared to me to be either semi-psychotic or psychotic as a result of the killing. I offered to try to talk to her as I can sometimes bring a generally normal person back to "reality" when they have recently slipped over the edge. The police officers refused my offer, however. I never found out what happened to this individual, yet I know it had to have affected her beyond imagination and I am equally sure the children have had major issues with violence and may still have to this day. We cannot be witnesses to experiences of profound violence without it affecting us in like measure.

On the first level of the Medicine Wheel the emotion of anger/rage is the most difficult to deal with because of the strong energy component. We want to do something when we are angry and that something may be destructive. Anger wants action!!!! Anger will become purified and non-violent eventually, when embraced. However, we need to commit ourselves to nonviolence or to violence that doesn't damage other living things during this transformation process. To hurt or injure living beings may cause consequences and it is best to avoid such behaviors. When our hostilities have built up and held in for a long time it will take a while to transmute and clarify. If it is overwhelming we may need professional help for a time, or even hospitalization, for our own safety and that of others, until it can be controlled.

It is practical for most of us in the process of working our way through our anger to choose some form of energetic activity to reduce the immediate need for destructive action. Many women will clean their homes at a fast and furious pace. Other people go someplace where they can yell or scream away from everybody. Some individuals may run or throw a ball against a building, some throw dishes or other items, away from persons or animals. It is okay to do most anything that uses up intense energy in a non-hurtful manner.

It is not unusual to get "stuck" in warrior mode because the energy itself feels good and powerful after the more passive energy of the wounded child. I used to work with many women who had problems with jerking or hitting their small children in anger. It had never occurred to them, when they came to me, that they could defer their rage until they used up the energy and then approach the child in a calm way. Of course, this works with adults too.

We get crazy inside and don't think clearly when we are very angry (or mad). Maybe that's where the term "mad" came from in terms of insanity? We become mad (insane) temporarily, at least, when we become really angry, enraged, or violent. We lose control of ourselves and make decisions that usually only make matters worse. For instance, when a verbal fight is started by one person in a family how often does the attacked person remain calm? It is difficult for one individual to continue to fight if the other person refuses to react. It becomes evident quite soon that the person who is ranting and raving or screaming is not in control of her/himself or the situation.

The calm individual is able to think and act as they thoughtfully choose. Too many of us in our world have not fully embraced the piece of ourselves which is anger/rage. I remember asking someone I considered knowledgeable years ago, "how deep is deep"? Where does feeling end and at what depth?" I now believe that we are capable in the deep wells of our beingness of unimaginable emotions under certain circumstances. I think few of us go to the far extremes, yet I believe the capacity is there. I somehow believe our capabilities for emotion extend without limit.

We sometimes turn feelings of anger on our psyches and feel depression when we reject anger in ourselves. There are always some slight indications that show up and let us know they are there if we pay close attention. We may also displace or project it on someone else who has no real reason to trigger that reaction.

Our primary task on this first warrior level is to honestly observe our emotions, dreams, thoughts, and behaviors. We need to determine what is happening with our warrior self in terms of anger and reactions concerning violence. It is the hardest of all directions and tasks, as it is the shadow part that requires an awareness which we may dread facing in ourselves.

Another task on this first level of the Medicine Wheel is to begin to observe how we use control over others and understand our fear of being alone. Being without a caregiver equates with death in young children and is one of the fears we may carry into our so-called adult lives. As we gain an understanding of our fears and embrace the frightened child, we begin to lose our fear of the unknown and of death itself.

The shift from other control to self control happens naturally as we begin the process of detachment and independence. The signs of control may be subtle. One of the major, sometimes subtle ways in which women in particular, use control is by holding on tightly. Persons with abandonment issues are especially prone to this type of control. It feels good to feel needed when one is fearful of being alone. Usually a couple will have patterns that are opposite sides of the same coin and they provide a balance for one another. If only one person grows in a relationship the other partner may become intensely clinging. Both persons will have to change or the partnership may dissolve. Most independent individuals choose other independent people as partners.

Abusive people are all about control. Men are far more likely to use more overt types of control such as intimidation, financial domination, or physical and verbal abuse. Both genders use manipulation as a control and addictive people are generally stuck in the warrior mode. Substance abusers are self-abusing and may also be violent when using substances to avoid pain or increase sensual pleasure. It is so crucial to our growth emotionally and spiritually to appreciate and celebrate what has served to bring us to where we are on this very day. I cannot emphasize strongly enough that it is only when we are able to embrace, without judgment, who we are right now at this very microsecond in time that we are able to make shifts away from our conditioned feelings toward the inner core of unconditional love and everlasting JOY.Punishments for the emotions we dislike don't work. We may use guilt to flay ourselves and the emotion may go away temporarily, yet it will be triggered again and again. I used to describe to my clients the emotion they rejected in themselves as a road block. This barrier would pop up whenever an unwanted feeling occurred. They would then punish themselves, usually with guilt or rejection. The feeling would then go away until some other event would occur which would elicit the same block. It would never be integrated into the whole of themselves until they accepted and embraced it. They found that when they were able to find the root cause and the emotion "huggable", it lost control over them and the roadblock disappeared.

We have learned a lot about ourselves in the warrior state and are looking toward the north direction as we find our feet headed that way, We may be loathe to move away from the action oriented warrior to the inner oriented feminine of the north, yet we find ourselves on the cusp and prepare for the drama and chaos we may find there.

North

We have begun our trek from west to north along the pathway toward a plethora of reactionary feelings and self-drama which may include egotism, attention getting behaviors, melodrama, exaggeration, arrogance and manipulation. It is extremely helpful at this point if we are able to see ourselves with humor and perhaps laugh at how clever we have been. If it is too painful at present, remember to delete judgment. It is okay to be wherever we are.

I recall when my children were little, that I realized I was making mountains out of molehills. At first it was quite painful for me to realize that I was doing that, yet it did not take long for me to see the humor and be able to laugh at myself. Other recognitions such as placing blame on others were much harder for me and I wasn't able to take responsibility and embrace that one for a long time. Embracing means finally taking responsibility for not only our own feelings but also our thoughts, attitudes, and behaviors—in other words for our lives.

The second, third, and fourth chakras are related to the north direction. They relate to fear, power, sex, control, self-esteem, creativity and compassion, and also to self growth and courage. In addition, we find other feelings such as pride, ego, sorrow, grief and shame on the negative side of the second and third chakras. The fourth chakra has emotions to be clarified as well. They include resentment, betrayal, grief, loneliness, abandonment and judgment. As you can see there is an overlapping of issues from one chakra to another and one direction to another.

There is a lot of work to be done on this pathway and sometimes we get weary. One of the things I am going to suggest that might be helpful to you to increase your self awareness is to watch a few soap operas. They include so much of the dramas that we often play out that perhaps you may see some of your own emotions and behaviors to work with, at least to a greater or lesser degree. If you choose to do this, ask yourself how these behaviors may have helped the characters get where they are today. Ascertain what might have played out differently if they had behaved in certain different healthier ways.

Another helpful activity might be to look at family patterns that you have observed and see how you fit into those patterns and how you might try a different behavior and see what happens. I grew a lot when my children were young and I could always see my growth outcome in them before I could see it in myself. Changing patterns consciously before clarified feeling is completed sometimes may help in the process and actually speed things up a bit. Use whatever means you can to help you on your way.

When I was growing up, my mother's brother lived in a big house in a major eastern city. It was a beautiful old house full of antiques and Persian rugs. My aunt Elva was a queen bee personality and insisted that she be treated as one. I hated to go to their house, although I dearly loved my uncle Dick. I was afraid to touch anything for fear I would get a fingerprint on it and my aunt would make me feel bad about it. We didn't visit their house too often as my mom and dad didn't like Elva much either. It hurt us to see my uncle jump to do her bidding every time she demanded something, which seemed to be quite often. Everyone loved Dick and put up with Elva because of him—neighbors, friends, and family.

All of us hoped that Elva would die first so that Dick would have some peace on this earth. It didn't happen. As they got older Elva would develop severe choking spells when she didn't get her way immediately. Dick, as usual, would practically turn himself inside out and she would recover quickly as he provided whatever it was that she wanted. You might imagine the feelings he rejected in himself, that stopped him from changing or getting out of the relationship. He must have punished himself with terrible guilt as he was a sensitive guy and guilt was definitely a family pattern. He was born in the late 1890's before we knew much about emotional change and healthy behaviors. Of course, we all blamed Elva not realizing that they were opposite sides of that old coin we have spoken so much about and that she was caught in the pattern as much as Dick. We weren't able to see that at the time.

Fear and judgment is behind all the negative energies and blockages of this and every direction. Our task is to recognize and observe and to begin to understand that all these reactions on this level are the result of conditioning and a lack of awareness. We are beginning to grasp the concept that it is within our own ability to heal our insecurity and all the emotions and attitudes that go with it. The pain and suffering may be intense for quite a while yet. We are beginning to accept, however, that it doesn't always have to be this way and perhaps there is a little lessening of the pain in some areas. Know that the fear will disappear with embracing and integration of our emotions.

Fear keeps us imprisoned in our own darkness. It is time to let the light shine in. We are afraid of losing what we may or may not have and feel jealousy and/or envy. We may feel betrayed by someone we had started to trust. Love is not involved although we may think it is. Desire for material or sexual objects may be a fleeting or sensual pleasure yet the heart chakra is unopened and unaware. Addictions have shame attached to them and may keep us from feeling our pain and loss. We realize that the anesthetic which addictive substances provide is a temporary analgesic, yet feel powerless to stop.

Some years ago I was working with a group of people with addictions in a hospital setting. One of the men I was counseling told me he was working on forgiveness. He told me about things other people had done that had hurt him and things he had done to hurt others. I asked him if he had forgiven himself for his addiction and he told me he had never even thought about it. He was so caught up in a cycle of pain and self punishment that he had never even considered compassion for himself. Persons who are blocked by their addictions need especially to give themselves gentleness and compassion. Punishment doesn't work!!!!!! As long as we are in judgment of our inner thoughts, attitudes, behaviors, and feelings, we punish ourselves. We must be able to see these activities as being servants and messengers that make us realize that we need to grow.

There are major issues of trust here on the first level and it is difficult to see from this standpoint how we can ever love ourselves unconditionally, let alone feel eternal JOY!! We feel that we need to get ahead of ourselves and delete these emotions before we can even think of ourselves as being worthy of love. We cannot go at it backwards, however. It is still necessary to embrace the feelings, hug ourselves and appreciate how all this mass of energy/emotion have brought us right here where we are.

East

We move now toward the east direction, the one in which the sun rises. Hopefully we are beginning to see the light as we walk on this final pathway on the first level of the Medicine Wheel. Remember that we can move backward as well as forward, and down as well as up. It may seem that we have entirely embraced an emotion only to find that some event (inner or outer) has triggered it again and we need to revisit the appropriate place on the Medicine Wheel and work on it some more.

We have arrived at the place of judgment, the place of our "stuff" and the heart which has not been opened to loving ourselves. We are all moving in the same direction, yet sometimes we are blocked because of our fears which hold us in bondage. Our fear causes us to put "blinders" on our eyes so that we believe there is only the world that we know and are more or less comfortable with. The curtains over our eyes keep us from seeing the world and universes beyond our self-limiting vision; yet they are there.

Judgment is based on a hierarchal system which gives authority to institutions or individuals and gives them power over other people. It involves comparison, separation, competition, and control. For us it starts with our parents or caregivers who define the world for us, who tell us "no", and that we must obey them for our own safety, survival, and nourishment. While this is usually not stated in so many words, we get the message. Our parents are our models, and if they never question the authority of government, school, church, doctors, lawyers, and Indian chiefs, then we usually learn that authority is not to be questioned. We may, in fact, see authority as dictatorial: We may be afraid of it.

On the other hand, if our parents are open and questioning, we learn that it is okay to question. We do not have to believe blindly in any belief system or way of life, and we are not fearful of authority figures. We perceive that God, as we understand the concept, can be experienced on a personal level and may not be what we have been told by someone else, however well meaning. We are able to choose to follow laws or whatever else is required of us legally or otherwise, either because of the consequences if we don't, or because we believe it is best for us and the community of humanity that we interact with and are a part of.

Judgment is a large part of the hierarchal system with its higher and lower ranks. I have portrayed the extreme ends of that system yet most of us fall somewhere in between. How many of us as humans have not had to struggle with authority issues? How many of us have not had control problems? How many of us have not made comparisons of ourselves to others? I would venture to say that probably all of us have been intimidated at one time or another by an authority figure.

We are most certainly caught up in our own judgments on this first level of the Inca Medicine Wheel as a reaction to a multitude of events. Practically everything we think about is marred by comparison. On the one hand we nearly always feel inadequate in a hundred thousand ways, and these become a hundred thousand ways we can feel unworthy of love. We can always find someone who is brighter, funnier, prettier, stronger, more whatever than we are. We may also feel we are superior, (which is the opposite polarity), and therefore part of the same pattern. In such case there will always be the fear that someone will come along who will take our superior feeling of power away. The real power of unconditional love and JOY eternal can never, ever be taken from us.

When we are truly secure, we feel neither inferior nor superior to anyone else. There is no ego involved, and no feelings of competition. We feel equal and friendly to others. There is no need for subservience or arrogance and it doesn't arise. We know deep down that we are loveable and worthy of that love. It is hard to perceive that we will never need or want to be "first" or "best". It just happens this way when we delete judgment.

Until we reach the point of equality we need to pay close attention and observe our self put-downs and competitive/comparative thinking and emotion. Do not accept self-judgment!!!! We need to tell ourselves that we don't have to go "there". Embrace ourselves and delete, delete,

delete. Judgment has helped us to survive in a crazy and negative world, and we don't need it any more. Try to catch and understand the subtle putdowns, because they may be the ones that block our passage the most.

For some reason I have always been certain that God is an unconditionally loving and nonjudgmental being. This did not stop me from being judgmental about myself to the nth degree. My parents were more democratic than most, yet there were limits to the embracement of the emotional shadow parts of themselves and those were passed on to my sister and me.

We need to realize as we go along our journey that each of us is incredibly beautiful, to peer through the negativity to see within ourselves the Holy Grail, the pure shining core of unconditional love and JOY that is everlasting!!! It is here in each of us, and if we can begin, on this first level of the Medicine Wheel, to look beyond that which covers and clouds the sun of our central being, then we have prepared ourselves to ascend to the next level. With our new found awareness and observation we have already begun to clarify our emotions and the transformation process is under way.

I believe that if we could just "click" our inner mouse and erase all of our judgmental emotions, in one fell swoop, we would clear away all our fears, negative emotions, and insecurity and we would be free. Some day I hope to discover a "key" that will quickly and easily remove judgment from our inner being.

Before we move on to the second level of the Inca Medicine Wheel I would like to suggest that meditation would be helpful as a tool in raising vibrations. I always found early morning best for me when I first started, before the turmoil of the day began. Visualizing our pure white, light core self and focusing on its vibrations is sure to bring us comfort if we practice conscientiously over a period of time.

CLARIFYING THE EMOTIONS

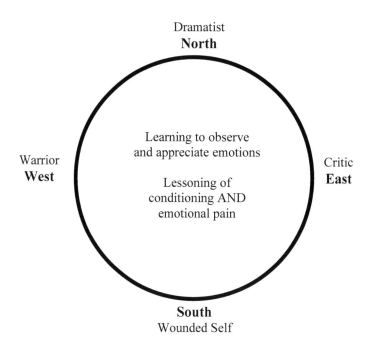

Dramatist
North

Warrior
West

Learning to observe
and appreciate emotions

Lessoning of
conditioning AND
emotional pain

Critic
East

South
Wounded Self

LEVEL II

LEVEL II: Clarifying the Emotions

As we move forward we have come full circle around the Inca Medicine Wheel and are now on the second level. We have been working diligently with our reactionary feelings, and are no longer at their mercy. Our feelings at this point are sometimes still strong and painful, and we haven't embraced them fully. But we do have some control over them and don't react blindly when they appear. The task on this level of the wheel is to provide a cleansing process of the first four chakras and to finally open up the heart to unconditional love.

At the beginning of this phase we are starting to access the "healer" within. In Inca terms this part of the self is still wounded, yet is also responsible for, and capable of, cleansing and healing the pain and suffering caused from unacceptable emotions, thoughts, attitudes, and actions. The self has received a wake-up call that allows him/her to recognize that there is the potential within the self for comfort and growth. The self is now generally able to observe the inner processes and to analyze and interpret what is happening on a feeling level, as it occurs.

This is an interesting and exciting process as we learn and see the changes, not only in ourselves but also in others who are responding to those changes. This is an excellent time to keep a dream journal, as well as, a regular daily diary of what is occurring, if you haven't already started. We can often see much more clearly from these helpful writings than from intellectual observations only. I would strongly encourage you to make this a priority.

For several years I kept a dream journal and after awhile I would find myself analyzing my dream in my dream. I would notice some feeling I had not been aware of in my waking, conscious state, and I would say to myself in my dream, "Aha, so that's how you feel?"!!! I learned a lot about myself that way. Recurring dreams are of special significance. They are trying very hard to get our attention to let us know something we need to realize in order to grow beyond it. It is like someone keeps knocking at our door until we go and open the door. In order to interpret a dream, I put myself in every object or aspect of the dream. In other words, I become the object or aspect and analyze what that means to me. I am almost always able to figure it out. If for some reason it eludes us it will always reappear in another dream, or in another way until we "get" it. Our subconscious minds (perhaps helped along by our spirit guides) are so very clever!!!!!!

South

In the south direction we come again to work on our wounded, aching self. Insecurity is still a major problem and we may be feeling severe discomfort in particular situations, or we may feel awful most all the time for awhile. For a period of some months while I was going through this phase I felt like I couldn't get away from the terrible feelings. Sometimes when we are going through this consistently, it may help to have our physician prescribe some medication for a little while until we are able to understand and embrace our emotions.

Today there is more understanding about emotions and growth than there was back when I was experiencing the pain, so hopefully you will come through more easily and readily than I did. I believe my suffering at this point in my growth was due to my unconscious angry feelings that I wasn't able to accept, let alone embrace. I didn't know what was in my self, below the conscious level, and there was a mountain of anxiety that it might come crashing through, yet I didn't know what it was about.

For those of you who have had sexual abuse in your background, there is always rage. Unless we have told someone about it and have had professional help in working through it, the feeling will still be sitting in the unconscious, affecting every day of our lives. How can we not feel fear and tremendous insecurity when we have feelings we totally reject sitting below the surface of our conscious minds? Before I dealt with my own rage, I would sometime feel strong fear when a man would be walking toward me. It could be just any man who might simply be crossing a room and didn't look like the person who had abused me.

This is the time to observe yourself very carefully and pay close attention to what arises in you that seems to come from nowhere. There is so much in the depths and it can be fascinating to find out that there is a lot more to all of us than we thought there was, when we were simply reacting. It is also usually of great interest when we understand how we have used what we have experienced to help further us on our pathway, or when it has provided an avenue to survival.

The ultimate goal and task on this second level is to open the heart to unconditional love. We need to be super aware of the wounded child within and give him/her much attention; all the love, gentleness, and compassion that we can muster up. It is time to practice gentleness and caring. Most everyone is able to be compassionate with children, old folks, and/or animals. Often it is harder to be gentle with ourselves. Learn to give to the small being within yourself what you would give in kindness to someone else. Recognize the high price you have paid across the years in pain, guilt, and/or rejection. Wrap your arms around yourself and pour gentleness and compassion into your heart.

If you can't give gentleness and compassion to yourself just yet, do not judge or punish your self. Say instead, "Okay, I'm just not ready yet". My daughter had a special knowing about herself as she was growing up. I would say to her from time to time, "How about doing so and so?", and she would say, "Oh mom, I'm just not ready for that yet." I had to honor my child's process and you can do the same for yourself, and it's all right too.

We live in a world where we don't learn to nurture ourselves. Women, especially, learn to care for their parents, their children, their husbands, sometimes their grandparents and significant others. Rarely are we taught to nurture and care for ourselves. Men are usually given more nurturance by the women in their lives, yet by the same token they have not learned to nurture themselves either. Both genders need at this point in time to be intent on giving nurturing, compassion, and gentleness, to themselves. If everyone did this, it would be a different world that we live in.

Part of nurturing at this time of our lives is giving ourselves little gifts every day. They don't have to cost money. In fact gifts of the spirit allow us to know there is a higher power who is wanting to help us on our way. Things that I love as gifts often include beautiful sunsets, a bird, a special song from someplace unexpected, a flower in our garden, or a cup of warm tea offered by a friend when I'm tired; There are a million wonders outside and inside. Most are spirit gifts. It is up to us to notice and attend.

One of my greatest gifts of all time happened on an ordinary day as I was on my way to work. I was driving down a country road, as I liked to go the back highways, and see the countryside. On this particular day the grass at the sides of the road hadn't been mowed for a long time, and it was quite high. I noticed as I drove along that a big bird had landed in the high grass to my right, a distance ahead. I looked out of my passenger's window when I got to that place of dense greenery and just as I did, an immense American Bald Eagle was taking off right beside my car. WOW!!!!I can't tell you how thrilled and awed I was, and I still get shivers when I think about it. It was truly a gift of spirit that I shall never in this lifetime forget!!!

We need to take the time to "gift" ourselves—pay attention when we are outdoors in nature. This will help us "ground" ourselves to mother earth. The more attention we pay, and the more we appreciate and say "thank you" for the gifts of earth and spirit the more we receive. At some point on our journey we will begin to realize how abundant our lives and world have magically become.

Insecurity gradually begins to turn into self-confidence. It may occur in some areas of our lives sooner than others: social relationships or career situations, before close relationships with partners. Keep on embracing the feelings and crediting them for their aid to you. Give yourself the right to take the time that you need. Finally, on the upper limits of this level you will find that core of yourself, and unconditional love!!! Other negative feelings such as jealousy and envy seem to disappear as we embrace them in order to increase our feelings of security and self-esteem. I say again, take all the time that you need on this and any level even though you may come back to any place and work on anything which is not complete.

West

We walk forward now moving into the warrior space to the west. There is still a great deal of stored up anger and possibly rage in us. We are excited about what this segment of the medicine wheel is, on this level. We are learning to embrace the aggressive, sometimes hostile, violent warrior within us. We realize that an emotional shift has taken place or is about to take place. We are able to feel anger without losing control although we may need to still do something active to work through the warrior energy in the beginning stages of this level. Later we will be able to just observe it, as it arises, and embrace it.

We continue the healing process until we reach a point where we can usually just feel the anger and watch it go by, until it arises very seldom. We can then make a conscious decision when it pops up if we want to do anything with it, and we can choose how and what that will be. For instance, our spouse does something we don't like, and we decide that this is something we need to discuss. Our discussion will be open and we will not react even if she/he becomes angry. Neither will we blame, but take responsibility for our own feelings. It is amazing how well issues are usually resolved after we are able to be in control of ourselves.

This level in warrior mode is about letting go and changing our attitude about life. It is where we need to decide to see things from a positive perspective and look for the core being in other people, as well as in ourselves. This level is about moving the blocked warrior energy on both the conscious and unconscious planes. We may be in a rut because of the sense of powerfulness that is inherent in it. To move beyond this problematic energy requires not only observation, but recognition of the dynamics, as well as redirection of the self. Be aware that this can happen and make a conscious decision to move beyond.

Warriors are the "doers" of the Wheel and it takes effort to overcome the blockages, such as denial, and repression, that we may use as defenses. Continue to work with the healing model and use your dreams and whatever methods you have learned to help yourself.

There are other issues we need to address as we move along in this direction. Detaching is a hard one. We all detach from some relationships at one time or another so it is not something that we do not know how to do. In some relationships we tend to be caught up in dramas, manipulations, and power issues. We may be fearful of letting go. It may mean that we are afraid of being alone, as was mentioned earlier.

There is the basic fear that many of us unconsciously carry with us from childhood. The fear may be very strong and keep us in unhealthy relationships that we may consciously desire to release. I'm sure you have heard the saying that if you hold a bird tightly in your hand, it is always struggling to be free. If you let it go, it may fly away and never come back, yet if it does come back, it is there because it wants to be. We need to ask ourselves if we are the one holding the "bird" tightly, or are we perhaps, the "bird". If either of these situations apply to you, what would be your response?

We would all like to know that if we detach from someone we love that they will not "fly away", or if they do, that they will come back to us. The truth is we can never know for sure and that can be really scary. However, being the emotionally secure beings that we are becoming, we can survive without any one particular person. We may grieve but we won't be devastated if we are without her or him. We will attract healthier persons to us as we become healthy, JOYFUL, and loving. It cannot be otherwise.

Detaching simply means we don't get involved in the other person's life dramas and demands. We won't need them to give us unconditional love because we will soon be able to give it to ourselves. Our real need is to *give* unconditional love—the beginning of eternal JOY

Denial may be a part of the warrior path on this second level of the Medicine Wheel. We may want to believe that we are "different" and do not have the deep hostilities and aggressive emotions that are the shadow polarity of love and good feelings, in all human beings. Many of my former clients have said to me at one time or another, "I dislike someone or something" when it was obvious to me that they were feeling something deeper than mere dislike.

Usually these folks were taught that it was "wrong" to allow themselves to feel deep hostility, let alone rage, no matter what the circumstances. They may, however, feel tremendous anxiety and not be aware of the cause. It is on the warrior level that we may come face-to-face with resistance and blockage, believing we do not have the capacity for our shadow parts. We may have pushed all our deeply aggressive emotions into our subconscious minds a long time ago.

In order to begin to bring warrior energy to the surface, years ago I would make myself think of atrocities that I had read about in books or seen in movies that had horrified me. One movie in particular (that I remembered as a kid) had been unusually hard for me because of my general interest in, and caring about Native American cultures. It was, to my way of thinking at the time, the epitome of man's inhumanity to man. I believe it is a classic book, "Drums Along the Mohawk", that was made into a movie. It was terrifying with scalping and other atrocities, probably on both sides. I only remember identifying with the victim pioneers.

I would try to realize that I had the same capacities, and that given the same situation and culture, I might have participated in the same emotions and behaviors. Using this type of method I was able to raise my heart rate just visualizing it, and to bring back gradually some of my memories of rage and aggression.

If you have problems with denial use whatever works for you to bring your feelings and/or capabilities for violence to the surface where you can understand and embrace them. Eventually you will find your hostility coming through in some symbolic or true to life form, probably in your dreams. As I have mentioned previously, dreams are verrrry clever and present to us what we can't accept or embrace. They appear in ways that are disguised and portrayed in such a manner that we are able finally to accept them.

We are also working on becoming more independent on this second level. We will need to examine our values and feelings. We need to distinguish what our beliefs and values are as separate from our parents and significant others. If we have like choices then we need to recognize that we have evaluated for ourselves and not just adopted them because that's what we were taught. All of the tasks along the warrior path will be amplified if we come to it with significant aggressive thoughts, attitudes and behaviors. Be as cognizant as possible to where you are emotionally and spiritually. Take as long as you need to be on the westward path. There are no time limits. Give unquantified compassion to yourselves, as you are able, and no judgment.

The second level of the Inca Medicine Wheel may take a long time, possibly years, so don't become discouraged. Celebrate each victory, as every emotion embraced is a step forward. Somewhere along the way you will probably reach a point where you will feel contentment most of the time, and you will feel comfortable in your own skin in most situations. I came to feel a sense of well-being a long time before I became able to love myself without condition. The well-being would be interrupted when some event would trigger some emotion that I had not fully embraced. By that time it usually didn't take too long to understand what it was about and to embrace it.

There was a period of a few years where I felt as though I was on a plateau, with nothing much happening. I was content almost all the time. I wasn't sure there was that much more to do. Not a bad place to be!!!!! I have come to believe that the plateaus of life are not exactly what they seem. I have come to believe that underneath there was a lot going on, probably on the subconscious and spiritual levels. Of course, as we are prone to do, I created other lessons which I needed to become aware of, so that I could get to where I am today. Every small shift we make leads us closer to JOY without end.

Finally we have accomplished the tasks of the warrior mode on the second level of the Wheel, and are about ready to tackle the work of the emotional process of the north direction. We will be clarifying the reactionary feelings that we have been plagued by and/or pushed away from ourselves, and possibly our conscious awareness, for our whole lives.

North

The north is a very interesting place to be on this second plane. It can be quite painful to face ourselves in this position. However, if we can see the humor as well as the grace, style, and sometimes elegance with which we tried to control our lives and the lives of others, it will go a long way toward the healing process. We will focus on purifying the emotions especially of the third and fourth chakras; issues relating to control, power, self-indulgence and self-absorption, trust and the opening of the heart to unconditional love. That's a mouth-full and a large commitment.

All of these emotions are tied together. For instance, if we feel we weren't given enough love, food, comfort, etc. we are likely to feel greedy, wanting more. We may exert control over others so that we get our fair share of whatever we need and want. Our methods of control and/or manipulation may be very overt, or they may be very subtle. If we do get what we want, we may be unwilling to share because our feelings of lack and insecurity and our inability to trust keep us from feeling there will ever be "enough". Again, at least part of what we need to access and become aware of is unconscious. We need to be patient with our own process, until we are ready to embrace whatever is there.

The north is the place of dramas. We may exhibit all kinds of behaviors in order to get attention. We may, in effect, stomp our feet, throw a temper tantrum, run away, pout, cry, or intimidate in order to get what we want from those around us. We can even choke or hurt ourselves in other ways. The choices are almost endless.

I would suggest again that it is helpful to observe ourselves as well as to watch the soaps and analyze characters in books to see how we might identify with them. One of the very best ways is to take a deeper look at our family patterns. We almost always carry out the same forms of behavior as our parents did.

We even pick out our partners to match our own emotional shape. Imagine yourself as a piece of puzzle that is you. It fits who you are emotionally. You will automatically pick a partner whose shape fits yours exactly on an emotional level. As a couple you will look identical to two pieces of a jigsaw puzzle that fit together:

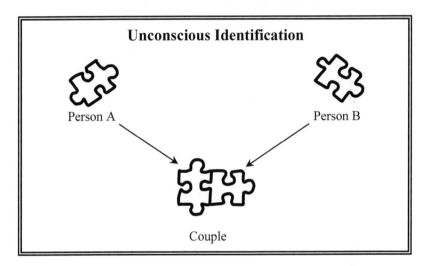

We usually have the mistaken idea that we pick our significant other because they are cute, or we like the same activities, or some other common reason, when all the time the "chemical" attraction we often claim, may come closer to the truth. We feel more comfortable with what we are used to on an emotional, mostly unconscious, plane. Each partner is a different side of the same coin. Can you see how the pieces make one "whole" when put together? We think we are making conscious choices, yet we are really prisoners of our unconscious patterns.

We change our patterns as we grow as an individual. If we are in a relationship both people may choose to grow. A partner can not remain the same if only one part of a couple alters the shape of their emotional pattern. It just doesn't work anymore. Both parties have to change or the relationship loses its integrity. Imagine one of the pieces of the jigsaw puzzle shifts its shape. Do you see how that affects the whole? I have known a few people who stay together in the same house when that happens, yet the "coupleness" is gone.

The more dysfunctional we are, the more dysfunctional our partner will be. The healthier we are emotionally, the healthier our mate will be, to the same degree. That is how it works. We usually marry the emotional image of mom or dad, at least on the first go-round. If you have had multiple relationships, think about it and determine if you or he/she haven't outgrown your former partners and caused the breakup.

All of us bring emotional "baggage" into our relationships unless we are very highly developed. We might envision a couple as the coming together of four persons: the adult person that you look like now and the "conditioned" child within that you bring with you. The other person also brings both the child within and the adult part of herself/himself. Hopefully we are each separately striving to grow our own inner child, yet how wonderful if we can help our partner when his/her elemental being threatens to overwhelm her/him. When we respond with compassion, instead of criticism and anger, we are not only validating our partner and giving him/her room to grow but we are also affirming our own inner self. Intimate relationships are tough because of all the old patterns and past events along with our genetics and present environment. It does get easier as we grow and become aware of what is really going on.

By the time we reach the third, spiritual level and have done the really hard work of the other two planes we have lost the pain and suffering and we are able to be JOYFUL together and bring a sense of play and profound intimacy into our daily lives. We see each other as individuals and allow each other the freedom to be what we choose to be, and we are also able to come together as one; worth all the pain of the journey.

Not all family patterns are unhealthy, so we can choose what we want to continue and what we want to embrace and integrate. Family patterns go back for generations often with little or no changes and probably lodge in our DNA. Many are very deep and very persistent. They can exert extraordinary power over our lives. This is the direction and the level to seek them out, and to appreciate how they have helped a family survive, over time.

I discovered a family pattern rather early on in my marriage, which gave me some misery. I realized I was acting out my parent's style of dealing with anger and argument. My dad would withdraw into himself when he and my mom had a disagreement. They never yelled and screamed at each other like some families do, and dad wouldn't speak to mom, except to answer a few yes or no questions. You could feel the tension in the house, like wading through knee-deep water, as soon as you opened the door. After a few days of the silent treatment mom would tell my sister and me that she was going out to visit a friend, and not to tell dad where she was going. She would always come back later that night. She was always back before dad went to bed, and he would be so glad to see her that all would be forgiven. They must have worked things out because there didn't appear to be later repercussions.

I found myself getting hurt and angry and withdrawing just like my dad. I'd say very little and be quite cool toward Ed. He didn't leave like mom did, yet we didn't resolve issues very well and so tension built up over time. Once I realized what I was doing, I decided I would stop withdrawing and talk things out. I did follow up on that but (and it's a big but) in talking things out I did a lot of blaming. It was all his fault (no matter what the problem). As a result he did exactly what his dad had done when his mom and dad had an argument. He would grab his jacket and take off, leaving me feeling self-righteous and furious. It does have a humorous side, yet I couldn't see it then. It was only after our marriage was over that I learned to stop blaming. I can say now that I understand his running out on me, given the circumstances.

I am including here an example of some of the work that occurs on the north level, mixed in with other directions of the Medicine Wheel. The emotions require clarification, and an understanding of the dynamics of the situation. The example also includes a recurring dream that was inclusive of almost all of the issues one person can have to wrestle with, and finally embrace.

The client was a woman in her late sixties who came to me because of depression and an inner tension that was causing her to be uncomfortable physically. The first time I saw her I was worried she might have a heart attack right there in my office; she was wound up so tightly. She had absolutely the worst childhood I have ever heard of, and I have heard many heartbreaking stories. There were all kinds of abuses including sexual, physical, and verbal, by *multiple* family members. She was able to remember only one time her mother ever held and rocked her. That was when she was little more than a baby, and her father hit her with a brick. She was doing the family cooking and cleaning by the time she was ten years old, and taking care of a handicapped brother, including changing his diapers when he was bigger than she was.

The sexual abuse had been forgotten, as she had repressed it long before I saw her. There was plenty of other material to deal with, yet I suspected there was more because of what felt like a giant spring that was coiled tightly inside of her. In spite of everything she had been through, this person was a very nice lady. After a few sessions I sent her to a massage therapist to help with her physical tensions. As sometimes happens with bodywork, it opened up her repressed memories, and she came in to see me with the new realizations. She was an emotional mess.

Part of what she told me was a recurring dream about a house of many floors. In the dream she could use the first three floors because she felt safe and comfortable there. When she came to the fourth floor she could not make herself open the door to go up, as she believed there were all kinds of fearful objects on the top floors that would harm her. We talked about the dream and over a period of about two years we worked with many issues. The final time she had the dream, it had shifted and she was able to go up to and through the upper floors, and, to her amazement, she found nothing to be afraid of. In fact, what she found was quite lovely. The upper floors also have spiritual significance as heights in dreams almost always relate to the spiritual level. By the end of her therapy this woman was able to function fairly well but she still had some issues to deal with on level two. She was just tired and needed a break. I moved to North Carolina and lost track of her at that point, yet I hope she continued when she was ready.

Another example of issues in the north direction relates to trust and abandonment, and the situation is not an unusual one. This particular circumstance involved an individual who came to see me in my practice when she was a young woman. She was the middle child of three with an older sister and a younger brother. She told me that her sister belonged to her dad and her brother belonged to her mother, and she belonged to nobody. When they went anywhere together she was left to straggle along, while the other four paired off. As a result her self worth was very low and her ability to trust was extremely limited. She was an unhappy person when I first saw her and wanted to be able to develop healthy relationships. She was bright and attractive, and after a little while she was able to shift away from the old patterns and finally came just to visit and introduce me to her new boyfriend.

As we near the end of the second level north direction we are almost ready to give up the blockages that have kept us from experiencing love given unconditionally to ourselves, and therefore, to others. We still have just a little way to go, and are feeling mostly good about ourselves. We are in control of our emotions and have mostly given up our neediness and lack of trust in who we are. We are ready to move onto the east direction and do our clearing work on judgment.

East

From judgment to unconditional love is a mammoth step with all that lies in between. We have talked a lot about judgment on the first level and are continuing to watch for any hidden signs of it and to recognize it for the major impact that it has on our everyday lives. Awareness is the beginning of the end. Do we still feel we need to compete for anything? Do we still compare ourselves to Miss Universe or Mr. Atlas or whoever men compare themselves to physically? Do we covet the 4 point grade average of someone we know? Do we still see things as good and bad?

The issue of judgment is a harrrd one, and we may find it sneaking in the back door most of our lives. We will probably always need to be aware and on the lookout for it. It is part of being human.

My sister and my dad weren't very close except that she could always talk to him on an academic level, and he was responsive to her in that way. I was daddy's little girl and got more overt affection. I felt guilty about it, because I loved my sister and wanted her to get as much affection as I did. I might not have liked it if she did, yet that didn't occur to me. What I did to promote their relationship was to not let my academic abilities show in my conversations at home. I was the social one who, while not brainless, did not try to compete on an academic level. Who knows, I might have been fooling myself all along and really *wasn't* as bright as my sister. This, I think is a good example of judgment, control, manipulative thinking, and self-punishment. It was subtle.

I always had some feelings of guilt relating to my sister. She was always tall and gawky as a kid while I was more average and people thought I was "cute" as a little girl. I got more attention than Marcia, and so I judged and punished myself. This carried into my adulthood, and it was in a dream that I analyzed in the dream that brought it fully to my attention, where I could finally embrace it and delete judgment.

Judgment is so hard to deal with because it is so ingrained in our thoughts. It is shifting, as we have embraced a majority of our emotions, however, and about to arise in its place is unconditional love!!! What we have been looking for our entire lives AND we no longer have to look outside of ourselves to get it. Love will come back to us in full measure because it is a universal law that what we give out always comes back to us.

It is such a reward when this finally happens, and it is a gradual process, not a sudden change from insecurity to love with no conditions attached. Every emotion, thought, attitude, and behavior that we have observed, understood, and embraced, takes us at least one step closer to this goal and to JOY as a lasting inner experience. When we have made a major shift and the light dawns, we may make a quantum leap.

Along with the final step in the north to love unending, we have also let go of the "emotional stuff" that we have been hanging onto. We have come to the realization that life is abundant and that God will always take care of us, in sometimes unexpected ways. Trust is not an issue anymore.

Twenty years ago I left the Hospice I was working for in the Orlando area. There had been a big upheaval in staff and I didn't want to be there anymore, so I resigned without having another job lined up before I left. I had just started going to Gordon Banta's psychic classes and he was channeling the Archangel Michael. I was worried about how I was going to pay my rent. I asked Michael what I needed to do. He asked me, "Do you trust us"? I said, "Yes", He said, "material things are nothing," I had lost my perspective, yet this brought me right back. It wasn't long before I found the perfect job with just the right people that I needed for that time in my own growth.

We finally reach the very far reaches of the east direction and the end of the second level of the Inca Medicine Wheel. We are happy where we are and we may be feeling JOY, some or even much of the time. Our vibrations have not reached the higher levels of the crown and throat chakras as yet, where we will feel the constant "hum" of all time JOY.

It is here I think we need to take a deep breath and give thanks to our God, the universe, the Inca civilization, and all those human and spirit who have supported us along the way. We have so very much to be thankful for, and this is a good place to celebrate!!!. We are approaching the final stage of our journey although it will not end until we become beings of light, and ascend into other dimensions!!!!.

SPIRITUALLY ENLIGHTENED BEING

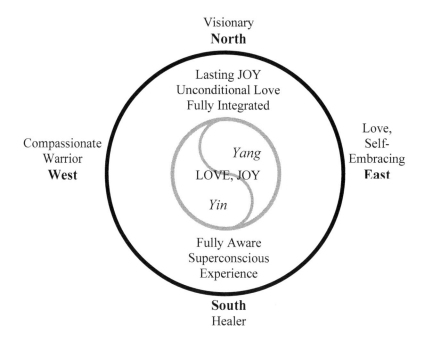

LEVEL III

LEVEL III: Spiritually Enlightened Being

Wow!!!! We have finally made it!!! The really hard work has been completed. Emotional pain and suffering are gone!!! If it is not, we still have work to do on other levels, and that is okay. It feels wonderful to be free!!! This is a level that we will surely enjoy and soon we will find JOY eternal, JOY that is never, ever, ending, JOY that is endless. We are on our way at this very moment. This level is about the fifth through the ninth chakras and the higher vibrations of creativity, truth, JOY, and BLISS and our connection to the sacred, to that which is God, whatever that means to each of us!!!!

Our tasks on this third level are to clear up any debris that may be hanging on from level two. We are doing the final clean-up job and purifying ourselves on the emotional plane. This is, however, just the beginning, as we are moving away from all our fear, including the biggest one—death itself. We have left most all of our old conditioned selves behind, and feel like a different person in the same body. For me it seemed like two different lives. I was one person up to a certain point when I became a whole other person who remembered and cared about the older one and could tap into the memories, yet it was like a definite split. Yours may feel different for you, or maybe not.

Many of us move into lives of service to others, if we are not already there. Even when we are not in a service related career, we tend to move toward helping other people in some manner, which heightens the vibrations of the whole planet. Some of us opt to aid those who are about to cross over, helping to resolve fears for the person or their families. Sometimes it is enough just to be there giving love, and gentleness. I would encourage anyone who is amenable to this type of service to volunteer some hours with a hospice in your area. You will find yourselves greatly rewarded if you do. Anything we do from our heart, to help someone, is also beneficial to us.

I learned early how much little things can mean to someone else, yet we often aren't aware of it. This was brought to my attention, very clearly, when I was in the fifth grade. Every morning on my way to school I would pass the same woman, whom I didn't know. I would always smile and say hi, or good morning, or something to that effect. It was no big deal to me. Somehow the woman found out who I was and got back to my mom that my smile and few words meant a lot to her. It was the first time I realized how something that we do, that is so simple, can impact another person—quite a lesson.

South

We have already entered the third level of the Inca Medicine Wheel and find ourselves standing in the south direction. We may be feeling a sense of awe for we have integrated all of our pain-filled emotions and are experiencing a radiating self-confidence and security within ourselves. How good it feels!!!! We know there are some straggling loose ends to be dealt with, yet we can look at them calmly as they arise, and quickly embrace and integrate without suffering!!!! Hooray!!! No more pain!!!! We have become a whole person!!!

We send out love to all of nature and to the universe. It is a gift beyond measure when we share our love with others from the very core of our beingness. Too often it is a rarity in all our lives.

One morning fairly recently I was walking down the sidewalk outside the town Post Office. A street person was coming from the other direction and as we got close to each other he looked up and smiled at me and said, "Good morning ma'am". All of a sudden I felt the Christ presence in him, and love literally slammed into my heart, like a bolt of lightening. It was a feeling of the most intense love imaginable, beyond description. I don't know if that young man felt anything like I did that day, yet he was gone before I could gather myself together to ask him. I am thinking that what I experienced was a bit of heaven. In fact, as I am writing this now, I am wondering if he was not an angel sent for the purpose of allowing me the experience.

The wounded soul and the wounded healer have now shifted into a healer in his/her own right. We can learn energetic healing which is universal and available to anyone. I learned at the conference I attended in Hawaii. It is described in detail in Brugh Joy's book, "Joy's Way." There are many books available if you are interested in hand's on healing. There are other methodologies as well. One is a computer program that picks up on quantum level energy and initiates the healing process within the body. There are also Egyptian healing techniques that are reputed to be very advanced. I don't know much about them and haven't seen them utilized. yet I know the ancient Egyptian civilization was very progressive. There is a healer, Kathy Russell, in Oviedo, Florida, who is using their Arcing Light methodology. (See appendix for website). David Harris is another gifted healer, (website in appendix).

On this level we are opening our throat chakra. We have let go of control and manipulation of others, and are able to speak differently. We have put our feelings of aggression and violence where they do not cause us problems, and we are finally able to be assertive. We come to situations where other folks might be either aggressive or passive, yet we are no longer in that position. Assertiveness may be difficult on level two and impossible on level one. Assertiveness as well as other emotionally developed behaviors become easy on this part of our journey. *Everything* seems easier to us now. We are beginning to reach our highest potential as human beings. We are becoming enlightened. We are JOYFUL about our status, and can hardly wait for all that is to come on this spiritual level. We feel a sense of excitement that we've come so far. We are having a new sense of "knowing" and of extraordinary experiences.

I will share one of my earliest major events with you. At the time it happened to me I didn't know about out of body experiences. I had somewhat similar happenings when I was a teenager, and I had forgotten about them until later. On this particular Sunday morning I had gone up to the front of the church to tell our pastor how great I thought his unusual monologue had been that day. All of a sudden I was outside of time and space. We were standing naked in a garden, and there was a sense of knowing each other completely, nothing hidden, and I had the feeling that it was unending. Then I seemed to realize I was outside myself, and was frightened, and immediately found myself back at the front of the altar. I felt more validated than I had ever felt before in my life, therefore I had to believe it was real. There was no way I could manufacture that kind of feeling!!! I didn't mention it to the minister for many years, and finally when I was further along on my own pathway, I told him about it. I asked him if he had experienced the same thing and he told me "no". If it happened to him (and I think it must have), it had to be on a subconscious level.

If you haven't had similar type experiences you have wonderful, marvelous adventures just waiting for you!!! Altered consciousness experiences become the "norm", and we hardly even remember what our lives were like before we became super aware. We move forward toward the west direction, looking forward to what tasks we have to complete, and what the shift to the spiritual warrior will be like.

West

As we move onward and westward on the third spiritual level of the Inca Medicine Wheel the self is becoming more and more integrated. We have finally become able to forgive ourselves, and others, only to realize there is nothing to forgive. It has all been about our creating situations that we needed to help us grow. If you haven't thought about this before, think haarrd about this one. We are not victims at all, if this is true, and I believe it is. Compassion flows out from us on this plane of warrior energy. We have become involved in one way or another in being of service or of sending unconditional love to other persons. The compassion is never ending and we are able to give to ourselves what we need as well.

Warrior and gentleness seem a contradiction in terms. They seem to be a paradox!! We are paradoxical!!!. We have now created the heart of a lion and the loving gentleness of a Mother Theresa. This is the true warrior energy of this direction and level. It is the well-known picture of the lion lying down with the lamb. It takes rare courage and undying commitment to reach the end of Oz and leave our cowardly lion, or the lion that roars, behind. The courage that we have paid an almost impossibly high price for, is real warrior mode and deserves an A+. We never need an excuse to celebrate and this is a good time.!!!

We have come to the realization that we are a part of a greater "whole" (think of the universe as holographic) and because we are independent now it is no threat to us; another paradox. We are whole as an individual yet do not fear the loss of ourselves in the exchange and interrelationship of vibrations. We can allow ourselves to become one!!!! We have made shifts based on the need to adopt new life attitudes that we became aware of during the west direction on level two. The position we are elevating to is extremely powerful due to our ability to love unconditionally. This is the strength that can never be altered; that draws like unto itself. Love is stronger than any other force. We are that power!!!!!!!!! There are times before we reach this core of love that we are more afraid of being power full than we are afraid of being weak!!!!! It makes us different from most of our fellow man. We stand out!!!!! It may be scary early on but now that we are here it feels good and "right". We draw other loving beings to us and create safe havens for others to find themselves.

We may, in this west direction, experience a life review (or set it up for ourselves if we haven't done so before), and also a small "death", seemingly a different individual than we previously were. Our unlimited compassion and understanding is the "gift" we have received from all the emotional pain and suffering we experienced on the first levels of the Inca Medicine Wheel. The west is also the direction in which we are ready to examine our entire thought processes for any patterns of negativity and to learn to control our thinking. We need to be cognizant of any tendency toward the negative within, and can tell ourselves, "I don't want to go there." That is usually enough to cause us to change to a positive frame of mind. The Incas saw this as a task on the spiritual plane. In addition to changing and managing our thought processes, our intuition is becoming more developed and we have lost all fear of change, the unknown, and death. We are also experiencing JOY much, if not all, of the time.

Manifestations of our spirituality alert us that we have moved ahead. For instance, we may find that spiritual music has been playing just below our conscious awareness, and finally comes to the surface. We may have spiritual dreams that give us insights. When my sons were small and before my daughter was born I had a dream that made a lasting impression on me. I dreamed it was "Judgment Day" and there were huge crowds of people. We were all outdoors, and everyone was moving in the same direction. I was with my husband and my older son, but Chip, my younger child wasn't with us, and I couldn't find him at first. We kept moving ahead and I continued to search for him, scanning the groups of folks. Finally Chip appeared, and he was in spirit form, yet I recognized him instantly. This was a dream that seemed to "slip through" though I was not on any advanced emotional level.

Another dream which was revealing to me happened at a time when I wasn't working actively on my spirituality. I dreamed I woke up from sleep and found I had been sleeping in what appeared to be a high ceilinged cathedral. I had fallen asleep on a church pew. As I awoke in the dream, I noticed how high the ceiling was and the beautiful light streaming through colored glass windows. It was bright and had a light, airy feeling about it that was altogether lovely. When I woke up the following morning, I *knew* I was truly waking up to a higher, larger sense of my spiritual self. This dream is, I think, a clear example of how our subconscious and spirit tell us what is happening on other levels of our being.

On this third plane of the multidimensional Medicine Wheel we are completing the work of integration of the male and female aspects of ourselves. This means that as women we can embrace the warrior parts of ourselves and become fully independent, emotionally and spiritually. We have given up control of others (the great illusion), and are in the process of final detachment from any other individual. We are realizing that we are our own authority, and we can decide who we are and what we choose to make of our lives. It is a fantastically exciting process to create the life we want!!!!!!!! We have already become our own healer, and now we can become our own author, editor, and publisher. We are capable of writing our own best script!!!!!!

This is an exciting phase for men also. Males are in the process of integrating their more nurturing, tender qualities, and emotions. This can still be difficult for many guys. The father of my children never rocked them to sleep, changed their diapers, gave them their bottles. How sad that they missed that from their dad and how sad he never had that intimate experience with our children.

I had many families whose spouses had Alzheimer's disease, when I worked with hospice. Most of the husbands became caregivers when their wives had the disorder, at least for a period of time, often several years. Initially I was surprised to notice how often the men became real nurturers, and seemed quite happy with their role. I know they weren't happy with the loss of the spouse, as they had known her, and the care was hard work, so I must then believe that these men who were not generally nurturing to their families early on, now had an excuse to allow that softer side of themselves to surface, and were pleased with what they found.

Thankfully, there are more men who are joining women on the journey to become whole, and forever JOYFUL. I have noticed that most women appreciate wholeheartedly the guys who are on their individual journeys. I am always, and in all ways gratified to see any man who is consciously on his pathway. On this third level of spiritual growth, men are becoming the compassionate warrior, relinquishing the final control issues and need for competition, comparison, separation, and hierarchy: rather than being weakened or diminished by embracing the feminine within, men become truly strong, alpha males as they become fully integrated. On the other hand women who are willing to become warriors and persons of action are also more able to surrender when the time is appropriate.

It is finally the time and the place where there can be true equality between males and females. Men and women at this level are able to bring the goddess/god energies as co-creators first within their own beings, and then in relationship. What I am stressing here is that first and always, of highest importance, is our own partnership with our own opposite gender. Becoming a whole person, integrating all that there is to embrace, makes us powerful. This kind of power has no ego attachment, and allows equality and true relationship between the sexes. Without equality one person is subjective and the other is dominant, and no one is a winner.

I suggest that women spend special time in the western direction on the Medicine Wheel, and men in the north. We need to embrace and welcome home the parts of the self that we may have rejected. The male/female/yin/yang aspects are also very much a part of the chakra energy, and the unblocking of these systems to higher vibrations not only leads to female/male union, but to enlightenment and JOY eternal.

We get ready now to leave the warrior direction and have observed carefully any remaining issues around violence, resentment, addiction, control, manipulation, denial, and fears of any kind. We are delighted with our positive feelings of unconditional love and the sighting of permanent JOY, humming away at our very core!!!! We are ready to proceed to the emotional north.

North

Wow!!! What a trek it has been up to this point!! We are standing at the threshold of the most sacred of sacreds!!! From here on we are illuminated beings. We arrive at the portals huffing and puffing after our workout in the west. Our eyes are on the last of the debris of emotional issues, and we find only traces of problematic feelings. We have embraced almost all of our "rogue" feelings and are so-o-o-o-o-o ready to reach the sublime.

We are having many extrasensory experiences and are at the place we can become the visionary, the shaman, the mystic. The differences are slight. To be a Shaman or holy person, requires total (as much as that is humanly possible) awareness of both the conscious and subconscious minds. The Shaman is able to leave her/his body and to search in other dimensions for a person's soul, and to bring it back to the individual's physical body in some cases.

We are capable of reaching out to other dimensions on this level and direction, and to receive communication from the world of spirit. We may just "know" with certainty information that is not available to ordinary consciousness. For instance, when I was twenty-three years old and had the toxic pregnancy, I knew with deep sureness that we human beings can take any situation in life and grow from it, or we can become angry and bitter. I was also certain that it was a choice of how we chose to respond or react. I made a conscious decision to grow. Nobody ever taught me that, I just knew it. This came through while I was heavily sedated and mostly unconscious, at a time I was in a lot of pain, experiencing unclarified emotions and wounded feelings. Probably this was the beginning of my commitment to my personal growth.

Later there was the absolute knowing that my purpose in life was to be a channel for God's love. I think one of the nicest complements I was ever given came from one of the residents of my retirement home. She had had a lot of problems and we had worked them out together, and she told me one day, "You treat everyone the same". She meant that no matter how anyone behaved or acted I was always consistently caring and did not have favorites or treat anyone differently than anyone else. That she was able to perceive this meant a great deal to me.

Besides just "knowing", we may be clairvoyant or many other types of extrasensory or extraordinary experiences with spirit. So many fascinating, interesting experiences!!!! I remember a time I went to a "past lives" workshop. It was a small group and we sat in a circle on the carpet. I was right next to the leader, and while we were doing a guided meditation, eyes closed, I felt a strong tap on my leg. I would have sworn the leader had touched me. When I asked about it she denied touching me, as did everyone else in the room. This was just one of many sensory type experiences I have had. Another time I was sitting on my young grandson's lower bunk when I felt almost a slap on my back. There was no one else on the bed and no one close enough to touch me.

116

I got up off the bunk and stood for a moment at its foot, and I saw what looked like the heat waves which come up off the street when it is very, very hot, moving from the head of the top bunk. It or they were coming toward me, and for a second I felt unnerved. Yet whatever it was passed right through me and, as it did, I felt a calm and warm sense of peace that hadn't been there before. Later I asked Gordon Banta about what had occurred, and after checking, he told me that it was the Archangel Gabriel who came to assure me everything would be okay.

The Collective Unconscious is also available to us on this third plane. It is the vast store of all information and knowing that has ever been. As I understand it, energy is never lost. It may change form, yet it is still alive and well; never gone. Gordon Banta is a good example. A professor from Rollins College in Winter Park, Florida once invited him to teach his course to prove he was able to retrieve information that he had never learned or studied. Gordon had a high school education. He was able to teach the class perfectly. After that he was challenged by a physics instructor to try to teach his very complex and specialized course. Gordon complied, and again was able to teach the material on physics. He always told his classes that the information is out there and that all we have to do is "tap" into it. Sounds easy, yet we have to be on the right vibratory level in order to do it.!!! I have heard of situations where this sudden acquisition of information has occurred spontaneously, and the persons involved were always awed and left with a sense of wonderment. Perhaps this has happened to some of you. It would appear to me that there is sometimes a "breakthrough" before we are psychologically or spiritually prepared for extrasensory experiences to come through.

On this third level, north direction of the Medicine Wheel, we will be accomplishing the tasks concerning communication skills; of speaking our own truth. It is here that we learn to speak with our spiritual voice. What you say may be inspired; what Brugh Joy calls the everyday self may become the inspired self. When I am speaking to groups I am sometimes amazed at what comes out. When this first started happening I was doing a lot of volunteer training for the first hospice I worked with. I would be talking away, and suddenly I would find rapt attention, and found myself in an altered state. I would find myself expressing ideas that I had never thought of before and had no idea were even in my head. You can observe that people think what you are saying is wonderful and inspiring, and it is fun!!!!! So go for it!!!! It's a great experience!!!!!

The throat or fifth chakra is about creativity, as well as communication and heightened intuition. It is our task here and now to stimulate our hearts and minds with creative thoughts and experiences. Try thinking about something in a new way. Write a poem or pick up a brush or pencil and create something new. There are books and other media if you feel stymied. My art and poetry writing have always given me great JOY!!! I never seem to run out of ideas. There are always groups or classes for writers and artists and photographers. In my next life I would love to be a wildlife photographer. I simply haven't had time in this one!!! I am lucky to have been invited to belong to a co-op of artists in Winter Haven, Florida called "Cracker House Artists." We recently started a gallery in the downtown area and have a support group of like-minded people.

When I was in college my friend, Jane, was majoring in English and speech. She wasn't impressed with the Tampa organized writers group, so she started an informal organization we called the "Splinter Group". It was made up of students, ordinary people who were interested in writing, professors, and a few musicians. We would meet at somebody's house once a month for a potluck supper and bring whatever we had written or composed during the month, and share it with the others. Everyone always had a turn reading or playing their instrument and composition, and the criticisms were always constructive and positive. We even had an 87 year old woman who was writing a novel!!! We all thought she was wonderful for fulfilling her dreams!!!! These gatherings were so fun and inspirational!! I learned a lot from that experience and I loved it.!! So look for creative groups if you are interested, or start your own.

The center of intuition and psychic perception is the brow area or sixth chakra. As we continue to open any blockages that have closed off our avenues to this point, we gain in wisdom and power. We are able to understand emotional and spiritual matters with a clarity which we could not have even dreamed of in the past. The old systems of our beliefs have shifted because they no longer make any sense to us. What has come in the place of the old ways may change again with new insights and awarenesses. We are prepared and excited about every new epiphany!!!! We are becoming enlightened. Meditation is an important pathway in every direction on this level of the Inca Medicine Wheel. It becomes easier and has more meaning as we move into the higher chakras. There are books and CD's with many fantastic guided meditations available.

Something else you might consider in raising your vibrations is to be a volunteer for a service organization. I found that in my work with hospice the staff generally has a high vibratory rate. The team leader of my team was a very supportive and spiritual person who set the tone for the whole team. The nurses were always and ever wonderful people with strong spiritual values. They give the finest care available, (all hospices that I am aware of), and they work long, often hard hours, giving gentle and loving palliative treatment. Almost always the staff and family form very close bonds.

Volunteers are much appreciated and treated as staff. In particular I remember one family where a teenage son was taking care of his mother who had terminal ALS; dad and mom were divorced. Another daughter who was still in her teens had come home with her baby boy. She took minimal care of the baby and did nothing to contribute to the family situation, except to make it more chaotic. The first time I came into the home every dish in the house was dirty and piled high in the kitchen sink. The laundry room was totally stuffed with dirty linens and clothes, and every chair in the house was covered with piles of "stuff". The little children crowded anxiously around anyone who came to visit, looking for affection and reassurance. They *knew* that something was terribly wrong, but they didn't know what. During all that was going on the teenage son brought his pregnant disabled girlfriend home because her parents had kicked her out. Everything in that situation was in chaotic disorder!!!! It was a shambles!!!!

After conferring with the dad, who had known his ex-wife since they were kids, he agreed to come back to the home and help. He would have the toddlers after their mother died. He was able to give everyone some stability and be there with the family. The most wonderful part of that whole experience was the volunteer who came in to help. I would come in the door and there she would be, washing dishes at the sink, with a baby on her hip, or she would be putting things away with two toddlers at her heels chattering happily away. It was not long before she had gotten the whole family organized and back on track in a most loving way. The volunteer in this and many situations is what makes the

BIG difference, although most situations don't require the time or energy of this particular family. If you think you would like to be a part of any hospice, it is a rewarding experience and there are many types of things you can do.

I would like, right here, to honor the CNA's that work for hospices all over the world. They are the "front line" people with each patient. In our organization they take personal care of from six to eight terminally ill persons a day. The work is hard physically, and it is emotionally even harder, as most of the patients, especially those who are on the program for awhile, become very much like family. Often the CNA is with them at the time of death. There is a lot of loss to deal with, a lot of grief. We had one CNA who had been with our hospice since she was twenty years old. For thirty plus years she has been nurturing dying people, giving them warmth and caring. In addition she was always nurturing staff also. I have told Pat more than once that when I cross over I intend to carve out a "special" niche for her, as I expect to get there before she does. I also told her that when that happens our roles will be reversed and I will do the nurturing!!!! Pat and all the other hospice staff everywhere deserve the highest accolades that can be given to them!!! I am convinced they are all old souls, even though they may not be aware of it.

Whatever is helpful to you in raising your vibrations is great. Music, especially inspirational music, is a great way to raise our vibrations. There are many musicians, singers, and composers who specialize in metaphysical music. Richard Shulman's (whom I mentioned earlier) music is divine!!!

East

We have arrived in every sense of the word. This is our final destination on the Inca Medicine Wheel, although we will not leave it, as long as we are earth bound. We are able to move energy up and down the chakras, although we will live mostly in the upper vibrational levels. We may go out into the ninth chakra at some point where we are not bound by time or space or psychological consideration. We may connect wholly to the creator/source which is an awesome, fantastic experience, no matter what form it is in.

The out-of–body experience I told you about was the closest event that I had early in my adult life. I have one other unusual happening that occurred just a few years ago. I was meditating, and soon I found myself on the other side. I felt that I was co-mingled with the Source. I was still aware of myself, yet I was at one with God and it felt wonderful. At the end of the meditation I came back to what we generally refer to as reality, at least I thought so. However, after that I would suddenly start to cry and I had absolutely no idea what it was about. The tears would just run down my face; Strange!!! After about two weeks when it was still happening, I called a psychic woman I had met in the mountains and explained what was happening to me. She said she would try to find out what was going on and would get back to me. When she called me back she told me that I had left a piece of myself on the other side and I needed to get it back. I meditated on it, although I had no feeling that part of me was missing, yet after that there were no more tears. There may be some odd and "wild" experiences waiting for *you* so be prepared!!!

Remember this is the direction of judgment and unconditional love, as well as JOY unending. Be aware that we may always be prone to subtle judgments that may "slip" through, just because we are human. We will, however, be living in love and JOY as constant companions!!! This is not a surface knowledge, yet is the profound sense of the inner core of our being. There is no way we can "falsify" the perception. There is no way we can see ourselves as anything except beautiful.

We will also be clearing any of the last bits of comparison out of our thoughts. We just don't go "there" anymore, nor do we have any major or even minor issues with authority figures. We feel comfortable and at ease in our own skins. We may tap into this feeling of comfortableness earlier on. We all have what my friend, Ed Carlson of Core Health, calls "the perfect moment". It usually happens when we are four or five years old, yet it may occur later. It is a moment in time when we feel everything is right with our world, and we have the proverbial "tiger by the tail" and JOY in ourselves. It is a good model to use throughout our journey to give us a clue as to what we can expect. Once we pinpoint that time we can usually re-experience it at will.

Now we are there!!! And all is better than well!!! Our spiritual feelings are alight and we continue to grow in mystical and visionary power. We may become exquisitely intuitive and prophetic, and we may become a shaman or "holy person". It is entirely up to us what we create for ourselves. We have the power to manifest whatever we choose for ourselves. We have made a decision to take the path that led to the eastern direction of the Inca Medicine Wheel on this third level, and now that we have arrived we can understand the intent that was made when we started on our way. Our intent has created all the situations that have led us to where we are at this moment in time.

As I think back on my own journey, I had the intention to be where I am today even though I wasn't quite sure where I was going. What I am sure about is that I created by my thought, intention, and visualization, the events that helped me to reach lasting, forever JOY.

New discoveries about the manifestations of physical matter are being made every year. It is an exciting time to be on this pathway and to have chosen to be alive at this time in human history. We are always able to set our intention, yet perhaps it is much more powerful at this spiritual level, and maybe we may be able to set our intentions to help our planet heal, and become peaceful and in harmony with all of nature. If enough of us create these intentions we may be able to accomplish miracles.

I want to tell you one more story of a miracle that I witnessed. It was a fourth of July in Pigeon Forge, Tennessee, at the community park. One of my artist friends had asked me to come and share her exhibit space with her. She was in that area for the show, yet lives in Florida, and wanted to spend some quality time with me while she was there. I have not been very amenable to arts and crafts shows (as this one was) because of the physical work involved and because fine art usually doesn't sell well at this type of show. I did want to be with Patricia, however, and so I agreed to participate. She was displaying beautiful painted glass objects and had her work set up on crates and boxes out in the sun because she wanted its light to reflect off of the pieces. We had no tent and it was excruciatingly hot. The only way I could stand it was to continually pour gallon jugs of water over my head, keeping my whole body wet.

There were quite a few people coming through the exhibits, but only a few were buying. Around five o'clock, when we felt like we couldn't stand it another minute, the sky started turning black and all of a sudden a huge wind roared through, collapsing the park's pavilion on top of some dancers, and tearing up every tent and structure and scattering every object of art and craft in every direction all over the grounds. It was a total mess!!

We were all in a state of shock and the rain started coming down in sheets, drowning everyone until we all looked liked drowned cats. We had to walk blocks to get to our cars in order to load up what was left of our sodden and unbroken mass of stuff. My car was parked several blocks away. As I was tiredly trudging along, I looked up and a sign on one of the shops I passed, flashed what looked like "Angels". When I did a double take, the sign said something entirely different. I couldn't tell you what, yet it looked nothing like "Angels". Of course, I told myself I was "seeing" things and I guess I was. When I got back to the park there were "people" who just "appeared" from somewhere to help us clean up and load up. The thing I could never figure out was that those of us working there that day were streaming water, and soaked to the skin, hair straggling, and dripping water, yet the people who came to help us didn't have rainwear, and they never seemed to get wet. When asked who they were, to thank them, they just replied that they were nearby and figured we needed a hand. I have always felt that I was being shown that those "folks" were indeed "Angels". I am wondering if we did, indeed, create them—a very good question.

Now that we have arrived at this place of light, love, and JOY, I want to say something about our transformation and alignment with the God source, and with the divine consciousness. By the time we are "perched" on this last and highest plane of the Inca Medicine Wheel the central core of our being is aligned, like the tires on our vehicles are supposed to be, with the sacred consciousness. We have always been a part of this consciousness, yet we were not aware of it, and like a jewel buried under a ton of rock, we were oblivious to its existence. Now our eyes are finally open and we are able to see that the core being that is us is also a holographic piece of the Godhead!!!!! We have taken possession of our divinity, without judgment, hierarchy, comparison, competition, separation or ego. All are equal and there is a comfortable humility that is without arrogance or subjectivity. We are FINALLY HOME !!!!!!

Everlasting JOY is an awesome wonder, a feeling of rainbow radiance in our hearts. It is a "knowing" that we were created by God, with all the vision of the creative process. It is the essence of pure being, and the underlying amazement of embracing our own worthiness. It is also feeling our connectedness to all that is, both in heaven and on earth. It is the comfort that comes in silence, and the beauty that brings tears of JOY to our eyes. It is the flow of unconditional love through us, from us, and around us. It is seeing the source of all things in ourselves and in others, and letting them know we are all of one piece. JOY is giving up judgment, and ego, and gaining calmness and peace. JOY is being able to let go of desire and live in the moment. JOY is perceiving infinity— endlessness—and allowing ourselves to *be* JOY. It is letting go of personal history and becoming detached from hang-ups, our own and others. JOY is the laughter that springs up like overflowing wells. It is our heritage and our gift. It is great fullness (gratefulness) and abundance. It is always here within us. It is the place where love forever abides. It is heaven and I have no doubt that it lives in each of us!!!!!!!!! WELCOME HOME, CELEBRATE, CELEBRATE, CELEBRATE!!!!!

APPENDIX

Websites

Ellen Spivey, www.joyunending.com

Ed Carlson, www.CoreHealth.us

Kathy Russell, www.arcinglight.org

Richard Schulman, www.richeart.music.com

David Harris, www.shunshentao.com

Anthony Edaakie, www.ceemrr.com/Anthony

Page Notes

1   Ayani, Jessie Estan Ph.d., "Kintui: *Vision of the Inca's, The Shaman's Journey to Enlightenment"*, Heart of the Sun, Minneapolis, 1995

2   Ross, Elizabeth Kubler, M.D, Death and Dying, Macmillan, New York,1969

3   Dale, Cyndi, The Subtle Body: *An Encylopedia of Your Energetic Anatomy.* Sounds True, Inc., Boulder, 2009

POEMS AND WRITING

BY ELLEN

JOY

Joy waits for no one,
Yet arrives
Humming
Upon the soul
Unabridged and unannounced.
Joy cascades forth in
Laughter
Cavorts outrageously
With butterflies
And wild "thangs".
Joy scents the air
With lightness,
Rising effortlessly,
Soaring
High above the clouds.
Joy dances exotically
And erotically,
Beguiling and enticing.
It floods the heart
Like warm honey,
Sweetening
The mouth
And like a
Lover
Embraces
The world.

Ellen Spivey (2008)

SPRING

In the autumn of my life
It is spring.
Green moss lifts beneath my feet,
And birds build nests
On branches that shade my head.
The sun shines warm upon my back,
And the breeze touches light
Upon my face.

Where has autumn gone?
There are no reds or golds
No falling leaves.
It is not time to reap,
The sowing has just begun.

I cherish especially the spring.
Green shoots, new life.
Let the old die and be reborn again
In every blade of grass, petal, leaf.
The cycle and circle of life
Starts, completes, starts, completes,
Birth and death,
And always birth again.

In my heart there is only spring.
There is no winter, summer, fall.
Spring, its hush, its days of soft welcome
Are forever here,
And I have <u>arrived!!!!</u>
I am finally here, at home in my heart,
In the center of my being
Forever green,
Forever new,
Forever.

Ellen Spivey (2000)

SOUL PORTRAIT

Down the deep canyons of my soul
Spirit winds sing to listening ears.
Green rivers flow and surge to falls that
Mist on rocks below, while quiet pools
Beyond, echo the colors of coming dawn.

Then......
Light bursts forth like a new butterfly,
All beautiful and golden, blending, now here,
Now there. with brightly wild flowers whose
Nectar is sweeter than anything.

High upon the canyon walls, the shadow
Of an eagle climbs, shouting her GLORY
To the wide air
Higher and higher, soaring the clouds,
Until... she TOUCHES
            YES!!!!
The   hand   of GOD!!!!!!

Ellen Spivey (1999)

LET ME BE

Let me be the JOY that lightens the heaviness of the world
Let me be the light that deteriorates darkness
Let me be the fragrance of the earth, wind and trees
Let me be the hands that lift and heal
Let me be the love that pierces despair to raise
Us up on wings of hope.

Ellen Spivey (2008)

RAMBLINGS
by Ellen (1994)

IF EVERS

If Ever 1

If ever I should sit on a star I'd look down at the world and
I'd see all these crazy people running here and running there,
Like chickens without heads, spattering their lives here, then there, and
I'd yell at them slow down, slow down. Yet they wouldn't hear me and
they'd keep forgetting to hold a flower in their hands or listen to a stone,
or touch the moon at night. Their lives would keep on spinning like tops,
faster, and faster, and around and around and they wouldn't know any
difference until they were wound down and couldn't go anymore.

And so I would stand on my star and wave my arms and hope to get
someone's attention, and I would try to think about what I could do to
get them to SEE and HEAR without getting down from my star. I know
I would really, really like it up there where I could see all of eternity and
I could ponder the universe first hand, and in the stillness I would know,
without a doubt, that being love and JOY is all that is important. Love
from a distance is still love, and nothing can stop it. I would send out
love and I would hope that some time, some where, a heart would open
and let the unconditional love flow in and although that heart wouldn't
know where the love had come from I would know, and that would be
all that mattered.

If Ever 2

If ever I should catch a rainbow in my heart
 I'd have to decide what to do with it. .
Should I keep it for myself alone, or would I want to share it? Would I
keep certain best loved colors and give the rest away?
Or would I share parts of each hue and keep a bit myself?
Decisions!! Decisions!!

I guess I'd like to think that rainbows are holographic and I could give a little piece to everyone and that little piece would become whole and I would still have an entire one for myself.

I'd look around and there would be millions of rainbows that everyone would be giving away and making into whole rainbows and the total universe would be full of the most beautiful colors; reds, blues, yellows, greens, oranges and purples, all pure clarity. Then I think I would have to laugh and laugh, until my belly hurt me, with unadulterated JOY.

And everyone would laugh and the entire world would be a joyful place because of one rainbow I held in my heart

If Ever 3

If ever I should hold
Your heart
Here in my hands I would touch it with fingers
Lighter than dew, softer than dandelion down.
I would be very still and listen to its sounds with my full Attention, until
I acknowledged every song
And every tear.
I would hold your heart secure in my cupped hands and warm Each cold spot until all the ice inside
Had melted.

I would look for wounds,
However small, and my tears would cleanse each one.
I would bind the hurts with
The softest ever gauze.
And I would hold your heart so carefully, for so long a time that, just perhaps, you would begin to trust and
You would begin
To heal
And maybe, you would realize
How great your worth,
And learn to live
A new life.

Dedicated to my daughter

ACKNOWLEDGEMENTS

Merrie Summey is here awarded my undying gratitude not only for her work as editor of this book but as a fantastic support in the "doing" of it. Merrie is one of the truly beautiful people of the world!!!!! Thanks also to my readers of the text and unequivocal support to Akara Stern and Pam Kunitz. I love you all and wish you JOY!!! And thanks to Joe Mercer and Anthony Edaakie for proof-reading and additional editing of the final product.

I would also like to give my thanks, love and JOY to my grandsons Robert and Bryan Berry who spent endless hours helping me with Charts, computer activities and knowledge that I simply didn't possess. Thanks again guys!!!!!

Thanks to all my family for all the months of putting up with me during the process of writing and putting this book together. I know they are glad to have me "back".

In addition I would like to acknowledge and thank the special persons who were "stepping stones" along my own personal growth pathway. I offer undying gratefulness to Fred Rumsey, John Tatum, and Gordon Banta who magically "appeared" when I was ready for them.

Also Marlene Houck, wherever she is, Richard Schulman who pointed the way to the Inca Medicine Wheel and to all the friends, coworkers, and acquaintances who encouraged me to complete this work. Everyone I have spoken to about it has said "When It is finished I want to read it. Let me know when it's published, I want a copy". To all of you JOYand CELEBRATION!!!!!!